ESP
综合英语教程：读写分册 2

主　编　李　显　宋礼慧
编　者　（按姓氏拼音排序）
　　　　刘旭红　宋桂荣　唐加玲
　　　　翟惠晶　张艳辉

北京大学出版社
PEKING UNIVERSITY PRESS

图书在版编目(CIP)数据

ESP综合英语教程.读写分册.2/李显,宋礼慧主编.—北京:北京大学出版社,2016.8
ISBN 978-7-301-23678-9

Ⅰ.①E… Ⅱ.①李…②宋… Ⅲ.①英语—阅读教学—高等学校—教材 ②英语—写作—高等学校—教材 Ⅳ.①H31

中国版本图书馆CIP数据核字(2014)第003475号

书　　　名	ESP综合英语教程:读写分册2 ESP ZONGHE YINGYU JIAOCHENG: DU XIE FENCE 2
著作责任者	李　显　宋礼慧　主编
责任编辑	刘　爽
标准书号	ISBN 978-7-301-23678-9
出版发行	北京大学出版社
地　　　址	北京市海淀区成府路205号　100871
网　　　址	http://www.pup.cn　新浪微博:@北京大学出版社
电子信箱	nkliushuang@hotmail.com
电　　　话	邮购部 62752015　发行部 62750672　编辑部 62759634
印　刷　者	北京大学印刷厂
经　销　者	新华书店 787毫米×1092毫米　16开本　7.25印张　250千字 2016年8月第1版　2016年8月第1次印刷
定　　　价	32.00元

未经许可,不得以任何方式复制或抄袭本书之部分或全部内容。
版权所有,侵权必究
举报电话:010-62752024　电子信箱:fd@pup.pku.edu.cn
图书如有印装质量问题,请与出版部联系,电话:010-62756370

前　言

随着《国家中长期教育改革和发展规划纲要(2010—2020)》的颁布实施，大学英语教学面临着更为严峻的挑战。制订中的《大学英语教学指南》将大学英语教学内容分为通用英语、专门用途英语和跨文化交际三个部分，并指出："专门用途英语课程凸显大学英语工具性特征。各高校应以需求分析为基础，根据学校人才培养规格和学生需要开设体现学校特色的专门用途英语课程。"同时，在高考英语社会化的推动下，通用英语课程的社会化也在紧锣密鼓的推进中。《ESP综合英语教程：读写分册2》正是在这种大形势下，结合齐鲁工业大学为代表的应用型地方理工类高校的要求编写而成的。

该教材涵盖面广，选材丰富，是集科学性、实用性、针对性为一体的一套大学英语教材，主要为已经通过大学英语四级考试的学生和有进行涉外工作需求的学生准备。本教材出版前，以讲义的形式在齐鲁工业大学2012—2015级的国际班及2014级B班中进行了试用，并进行了反复的修改。

该教材的特色主要体现为：

1. 实用性

教材以职场的日常所需为主要内容，涉及范围广，在提供所需基本词汇和表达法的基础上，综合培养学生的职场英语交际能力，满足应用型高校学生的需求。

2. 针对性

教材有着很强的针对性，即针对英语已经达到了相当于大学英语四级水平，并且有志于从事涉外职业的英语学习者。

3. 衔接性

教材特别注重通用英语与专业英语的衔接，旨在让学生在开始专业英语学习之前，对职场英语有一个比较全面的认识，而对与本专业相关的英语只做初步的介绍和引导。

本书编写过程中，得到了齐鲁工业大学教务处和外国语学院的大力支持和帮助，其他有关学院的专家也对教材的选材进行了指导。而齐鲁工业大学四年来使用该教材的数百名学生，对于教材的最终完善成稿也做出了很大的贡献，在此一并表示感谢。

由于水平有限，书中疏漏之处在所难免，恳请广大专家、读者批评指正。

编　者
2016年5月

Contents

Unit 1　Company Introduction 1
　　Unit Aims 1
　　Warming Up 1
　　I. Introducing Background Information to the Visiting Customer ... 1
　　II. Making Introductions 3
　　III. Company Target 5
　　IV. Practicing 6
　　V. Optional Reading 7

Unit 2　Product Introduction 9
　　Unit Aims 9
　　Warming Up 9
　　I. Presenting Products 9
　　II. How to Creat a Product Presentation 13
　　III. Strategies of Product Introduction 15
　　IV. Practicing 16
　　V. Optional Reading 17

Unit 3　Marketing 21
　　Unit Aims 21
　　Warming Up 21
　　I. Marketing Survey and Target Audience 21
　　II. Market Strategy, Advertising and Promotion 23
　　III. Marketing 26
　　IV. Practicing 28
　　V. Optional Reading 30

Unit 4 Purchase Order 33
   Unit Aims 33
   Warming Up 33
   I. Place a Purchase Order 33
   II. How to Create a Purchase Order 36
   III. Purchase Order Conditions 39
   IV. Practicing 41
   V. Optional Reading 44

Unit 5 Finance 45
   Unit Aims 45
   Warming Up 45
   I. The American Financial System 45
   II. Opening a Savings Account 47
   III. The International Monetary Situation 49
   IV. Practicing 51
   V. Optional Reading 51

Unit 6 Business Plan 54
   Unit Aims 54
   Warming Up 54
   I. Business Plan Writing 54
   II. What Is a Business Plan 55
   III. Reading 56
   IV. Practicing 59
   V. Optional Reading 62

Unit 7 The Financial Statement 64
   Unit Aims 64
   Warming Up 64
   I. The Balance Sheet 64
   II. The Income Sheet 67
   III. The Cash Flow Statement 68
   IV. Practicing 70
   V. Optional Reading 71

Contents

Unit 8 E-commerce **75**
    Unit Aims 75
    Warming Up 75
    I. How to Shop Online 75
    II. What Is E-commerce? 76
    III. Reading 77
    IV. Practicing 80
    V. Optional Reading 81

Unit 9 Business Meeting **84**
    Unit Aims 84
    Warming Up 84
    I. Setting up and Canceling Meetings 84
    II. Meeting Procedure 86
    III. Meeting Discussions 89
    IV. Taking Meeting Minutes 91
    V. Meeting Agenda 92
    VI. Practicing 93
    VII. Optional Reading 94

Unit 10 Board Meeting **96**
    Unit Aims 96
    Warming Up 96
    I. How to Run a Board of Directors Meeting 96
    II. How to Conduct a Board of Directors Meeting 97
    III. Board of Directors Meeting Rules 99
    IV. Practicing 100
    V. Optional Reading 101

Unit 1   Company Introduction

Unit Aims

- To master the basic knowledge about how to introduce a company
- To master the basic expressions about company introduction
- To make an impressive company introduction independently to different customers

Warming Up

Company introduction is the first step to establish business relationship with potential customers. Therefore an impressive company introduction can help get out the basic information regarding your company such as who you are, what your business offers and so on. With your partner, find a company introduction on the Internet, and then figure out what is the basic information included in a company introduction. The first one is given below.

I. Introducing Background Information to the Visiting Customer

Read the dialogue between the company representative Jack and the visiting customer Joan Smith. Then talk about the basic information of the company with your partner.

Joan: Could you give me some information about your company?
Jack: Of course. Our company was established in 1987. We mainly deal in the manufacture and sales of furniture.
Joan: What is your organizational structure?
Jack: Our company consists of four departments: Production, Finance, Marketing and Research & Development.
Joan: How many people work for your company?

Jack: We have about 600 people worldwide, and there are 400 workers here in the factory.

Joan: Good. You see, we have interest in establishing a joint venture with a Chinese partner. It seems that your company is one of our choices. But what I'd like to know is about your financial standing.

Jack: I can assure you that we have a very sound financial standing. You can consult our bank, the Bank of China, Shenzhen.

◎ Useful Expressions

◎ When talking about company history you may hear:

How long have you been on this site?

When was your company set up?

When was your company established?

When did you start operation?

I want to know more about your company history.

Could you tell me a few things about the history of your company?

I would appreciate it if you can tell me something about your company history.

◎ When talking about company history you may say:

We moved here five years ago. Before that, we were in a very small office building in the center of the town.

Ten years ago—by Simon Donna who is still the managing director. He started the company with just two people.

We were established in 1997.

We started operation in early 2005.

We began selling rice cookers from one small shop in Taipei. At that time, we were strictly a mom-and-pop operation.

It has a history of ... years, which makes it the oldest factory in our region.

◎ When talking about company business activities you may say :

We are in ... business.

We provide ... service for our customers for about 15 years.

We are mainly engaged in the manufacturing and sales of ...

We mainly trade in...

We have been manufacturing... for 15 years now.

We are one of the most important private enterprises specialized in ...

We run a so-called "shopping-search" website.

Unit 1 Company Introduction

We are the second largest manufacturer of ...

◎ *When talking about company culture you may say:*
With the development of economic globalization and market economy, our company sets "scientific development theory" as our guidance, enhances reform and transforms enterprise operation development mode with the goal of developing its main business, improving core competitive strength, and becoming one of the leading enterprises in this field.

employee commitment
fully empowered employees
high integrity workplace
strong trust relationships
highly effective leadership
effective systems and processes
performance-based compensation and reward programs
customer-focused
effective 360-degree communications
commitment to learning and skill development
emphasis on recruiting and retaining outstanding employees
high degree of adaptability
high accountability standards
demonstrated support for innovation

II. Making Introductions

Read the following dialogue and talk about the company development with your partners.

Tips
When we talk about company development, it will convince the customers if we give them specific figures.

A: I would like to know more about your company.
B: Our company was established in 1978. It is now one of the biggest manufacturers of the transportation equipment. We are engaged in a wide range of related products. The annual output value reached one hundred million *Yuan* last year, that is, about 13 million in U.S. dollars.
A: How many workers do you have now?
B: About 2,300 in factories and 600 in offices.

A: What is your market share?
B: Now we have 20% of the market.
A: What about your capital?
B: Our registered capital is 20 million *Yuan*. We were listed on the Shanghai Stock Exchange one year ago, and presently we have a market capitalization of 50 million *Yuan*.
A: Very impressive. Thank you for your information.
B: Not at all. We look forward to your positive reply.

◎ Useful Expressions

Market share

Market-share maintenance

Market-share threshold

Market-share leadership

What is your market share?

We now have about 40% of the market.

We have a market capitalization of $15 billion.

Our turnover is ...

Our sales is ...

The products produced by our company are well received in as many as over 20 provinces and cities around the country and enjoy a good market in Southeast Asia and (countries in) Eastern Europe as well.

In its traditional computing market, Apple continues to maintain its position as a leading innovator, strengthening its range of high quality laptop and desktop products. This has led to total Mac unit sales growing to over 7m and delivering $10.3bn of core revenues in 2007—an increase of 40% on 2006.

In fact, our appliances are used in one out of three households in Taipei.

As a matter of fact, you'll find at least one Action appliance in one out of three households in Taipei alone.

III. Company Target

Read the following passage about Sinopec Group and pay attention to the last part of the passage and talk about it with your partner.

China Petrochemical Corporation (Sinopec Group) is a super-large petroleum and petrochemical enterprise group established in July 1998 on the basis of the former China Petrochemical Corporation. Sinopec Group is a state-owned company solely invested by the State, functioning as a state-authorized investment organization in which the state holds the controlling share. Headquartered in Beijing, Sinopec Group has a registered capital of RMB 182 billion. In 2011 it ranked as the 5th largest company in sales in *Forbes Global 2000*. In 2009, it was ranked 9th by Fortune *Global 500*, becoming the first Chinese corporation to make the top ten and in 2010 it was ranked 7th. In 2007, it ranked first in the Top 500 Enterprises of China ranking.

Sinopec Group is one of the largest integrated energy and chemical company in China. The scope of its business mainly covers oil and gas exploration and production, extraction, pipeline transmission and marketing; oil refining; production, marketing, storage and transportation of petrochemicals, chemical fibers, chemical fertilizers and other chemical products; import, export and import/export agency business of crude oil, natural gas, refined oil products, petrochemicals, chemicals, and other commodities and technologies; research, development and application of technology and information. The company is China's largest producer and supplier of refined oil products (including gasoline, diesel and jet fuel, etc.) and major petrochemical products (including synthetic resin, synthetic fiber monomers and polymers, synthetic fiber, synthetic rubber, chemical fertilizer and petrochemical intermediates). It is also China's second largest crude oil producer.

As an endeavor to become a multinational energy and chemical company with fairly strong international competitiveness, Sinopec Group will seriously implement strategies of resource, market, integration and internationalization with more focus on innovation of science, technology and management expertise, as well as improvement of employees' quality.

Tips

The last part of the company introduction usually expresses company target, goodwill and hope. Sometimes this part can be omitted.

Examples:

Recent consumer research leads us to believe that a market exists in Canada and the States for our appliances.

Marketing studies show that a market exists in Canada and the States for our compact products.

Going forward, Google is targeting the mobile space.

This is all ample evidence to highlight that innovation in Apple is not hype: Apple really delivers its goal to provide "innovative integrated digital lifestyle solutions" and is a company that consistently demonstrates the power of innovation in driving profitable, sustained growth.

I hope that ...

ABC will initiate the second phase of our development strategy. Our company regards "reasonable prices, efficient production time and good after-sales service" as our tenet. We hope to cooperate with more customers for mutual development and benefits. We welcome potential buyers to contact us.

IV. Practicing

1. Match the English words and phrases with the proper Chinese meanings.

(1) 市场份额　　　　　　　a. turnover
(2) 注册资本　　　　　　　b. sales
(3) 年贸易额　　　　　　　c. core revenues
(4) 市场资本　　　　　　　d. market capitalization
(5) 纯利润　　　　　　　　e. market share
(6) 年度生产总值　　　　　f. annual trading value
(7) 销售额　　　　　　　　g. registered capital
(8) 核心收入　　　　　　　h. annual output value
(9) 营业额　　　　　　　　i. net profit
(10) 年产量　　　　　　　 j. annual production

2. Translate the following English words and phrases into Chinese.

(1) a trading company　　　　　　_____
(2) a public limited company　　　_____

(3) a private limited company _____
(4) a stock company _____
(5) agents _____
(6) suppliers _____
(7) a state-owned corporation _____
(8) a service provider _____
(9) contractors _____
(10) importers and exporters _____

3. Fill in the blanks with the following words and phrases.

| has evolved into | specialized in | listed | guarantee | comply with |

(1) After 30 years' operation, CELEC _____ a comprehensive enterprise, extending its business scope from international trade to overseas engineering.
(2) ABC company has been _____ among the largest 30 contractors in the world by a famous US magazine.
(3) Established in 1990, Action company is a manufacturer _____ the research, development and production of household appliances.
(4) All of our products _____ international quality standards and are well appreciated in a variety of markets throughout the world.
(5) Our well-equipped facilities and excellent quality control system throughout all stages of production enable us to _____ total customer satisfaction.

V. Optional Reading

In its traditional computing market, Apple continues to maintain its position as a leading innovator, strengthening its range of high quality laptop and desktop products. This has led to total Mac unit sales growing to over 7m and delivering $10.3bn of core revenues in 2007—an increase of 40% on 2006. Allied to this, the iPod range has been extended with the new iPod Touch and an increased capacity for the classic models. Despite the average unit price decreasing from $195 to $161, there was an increase in unit sales from 39.4m to 51.6m, and overall iPod sales generated $8.3bn.

The launch of the iPhone created global publicity and cemented Apple's reputation as a company that continuously produces truly innovative, sector-disrupting products. With sales in the fiscal year of 1.4m units, the iPhone contributed only a small proportion of Apple revenues.

However it created huge consumer pull. Additionally the iPhone demonstrated Apple's ability to break through existing paradigms — it is sold at a fixed price, is linked to a specific contract and is only available through specific mobile operators. As with the introduction of iTunes, Apple has entered a new market and challenged existing business models. This is a key element of Apple's approach to innovation: while many see the product as the focus, for Apple it is the interplay between the product and the service that allows it to fundamentally change the underlying business model operating in the sector. First it was music and now it is movies. Via its iTunes service, Apple has challenged the way the music industry operates and the company has now expanded its music videos, audio-books, television shows, movies and podcasts repertoire still further with major links to all the key studios. In 2007 iTunes had its three billionth download and this helped music related products and services account for a significant $2.5bn of sales. Of course customers also expect a suitably "Apple" experience when they enter a store. And they get it. Apple now has 197 stores worldwide and this has redefined computer retail.

All of the above innovations have translated into corresponding financial success with Apple's share price doubling in 2007. Total sales increased by 24% to just over $24bn while net income increased by a staggering 76% to just under $3.5bn. This is all ample evidence to highlight that innovation in Apple is not hype: Apple really delivers its goal to provide "innovative integrated digital lifestyle solutions" and is a company that consistently demonstrates the power of innovation in driving profitable, sustained growth.

Unit 2 Product Introduction

Unit Aims

- To gain the basic knowledge about product introduction
- To master the basic expressions about product introduction
- To know the ways to present a product independently to different customers

Warming Up

It is not the employer who pays wages; he only handles the money. It is the product that pays wages.

Henry Ford (1863—1947)

(1) Name some of your favorite products. Are you familiar with the functions of these products?

(2) Go online to find what should be considered when presenting a product.

I. Presenting Products

Dialogue 1   Presenting New Products

(A= Miss Alice Wang, a Chinese businessperson; B= Mr. Miller, an Australian businessman)

A: Good morning, Sir. Welcome to our shop. Is there anything I can do for you?

B: Good morning. I'd like to buy a photocopier.

A: Would you please take a look at our photocopier on show first?

B: It seems quite common except for the design. In what way is it better than other brands?

Could you tell me about this model?

A: Yes. This one is our latest product. It was launched this year. As you can see it has an attractive design. Compared with other products, it is relatively small in size, light in weight, easier to operate, and the most important of all, it saves energy.

B: What are its measurements and weight?

A: It is 34cm wide, 56cm long, 32cm high, and it weighs 12 kilograms. This model has five colors available: white, grey, green, yellow and blue.

B: How many sheets of paper can it copy per minute?

A: It can make 110 copies a minute. It's quite fast, isn't it? What's more, this model makes little noise while in operation.

B: How does it sell in Europe?

A: It sells quite well in the European market. Now we're flooded with orders.

B: Oh, really? Do you think it'll find a ready market in Australia?

A: Sure, I strongly recommend this item to you. If you use this equipment, you can save 15% of your energy costs.

B: That sounds wonderful. Would you please give a demonstration?

A: Sure.

◎ Useful Expressions

(product) be launched	（产品）投放市场
be small in size	体积小
be light in weight	重量轻
save energy	节能
make little noise	噪音小
sell quite well in somewhere	在某处十分畅销
recommend sth. to sb.	向某人推荐某种商品
give a demonstration	演示一下
be flooded with orders	接到大量的订单

Unit 2　Product Introduction

Dialogue 2　Recommending Products

(A= Mr. Brown from America; B= Mr. Liu, a businessperson from China)

A:　Good afternoon, sir. Welcome to our exhibition hall.

B:　Thanks. You are exporting garments, aren't you?

A:　Yes. Would you like to take a look at the products on display here? We have just got in a fresh stock of silks, and we have a complete range of specifications for you to choose from. I'm sure you'll find the right thing you're really interested in.

B:　Oh, you've got such a great variety of products. Are they all made of natural silk?

A:　Yes. All the exhibits are made of real silk. The quality is excellent and the prices are quite competitive.

B:　Good. How are they selling in the overseas market?

A:　They are selling quite well, and enjoy a wide popularity in the world market.

B:　But which brand sells best? Could you recommend it to me?

A:　Sure. This Lover series is selling best in European countries.

B:　What is the superiority of the Lover series?

A:　They are fine in quality, beautiful in design, bright in color and superb in workmanship. Wear them on hot summer days, and you will feel cool and comfortable.

B:　That's good. How about these Taiji shirts? The designs are quite special and the cloth feels quite soft and smooth. Are they made of silk, too?

A:　Yes. They are also made of natural silk. The styles of these silk shirts are quite popular with middle-aged and old people. Every year we receive a lot of orders from our clients at home and abroad.

B:　That's marvelous. May I take some brochures?

A:　Sure, here are the brochures for the products. You can get all information from them.

B:　Thank you.

◎ Useful Expressions

products on display	展出的产品
get in a fresh stock of sth.	新进一批……货物
have a complete range of specifications	全部的规格都有
be of excellent quality	优质
enjoy a wide popularity in somewhere	在某地普遍受欢迎
be fine in quality	质量上乘
be beautiful in design	款式漂亮

be bright in color 色彩艳丽
be super in workmanship 做工一流
meet with a great favor in somewhere 在某地备受青睐
be popular with middle-aged and old people 很受中老年人的欢迎

brand value 品牌价值   brand identity 品牌认同
pricing 定价   branding 品牌定位
reliable reputation 信誉可靠 world-renowned 闻名世界的
win warm praise from customers 深受欢迎
have a long standing reputation 久负盛名
enjoy a high reputation at home and abroad 誉满国内外

I'll explain the characteristics of the product.

I'll explain it in detail.

I'll explain it in an orderly manner.

Compared with competing products, ours is smaller and lighter.

One of the excellent points about this machine is that it rarely needs servicing.

This model of ... is efficient and endurable, economical and practical.

The ... we produced is characterized by its high quality, compact-size, energy-saving and it's also easy-to-learn and easy-to-operate.

They are not only low-priced, but they are distinctly superior in the following respects.

This... will pay back your investment in ... month.

The new type of ...designed by our engineers is very ingenious and practical.

The maximum speed of this kind of ... is ...

Our ... are made of super... material and by traditional skills.

The ... are magnificent and tasteful and have long enjoyed great fame both at home and aboard.

As our ...are made of ... they are both portable and endurable.

As our products have all the feature you need and 20% cheaper compared with that ... made, I strongly recommended to you.

I'd like to entertain any questions.

During my presentation, please jump in at any time if you have questions.

II. How to Creat a Product Presentation

Creating a Product Presentation

Product presentation is an important part of selling a product to prospective customers. In many cases, this will be the customer's first introduction to your product and potentially your company. Proper preparation is vital to presenting your product in the best light possible.

The objective of the product presentation is different depending upon the target audience and the presentation should be adjusted accordingly. It is important to know your audience and why they are interested enough to hear your presentation.

Factors to consider

Objective—What's the purpose of your presentation? Is it to inform, persuade, or entertain?

Target audience—Who are you giving the presentation to? What are their needs and immediate concerns? What are their individual goals?

Orientation—How much does your audience know of your product and other similar products? What is special about the way this audience looks at your product? Do they have any preconceived notions? What are their special interests?

Target presenter—Who will be giving the presentation? (Yourself, a sales person, a company executive?)

It is helpful to write the above information down before building the product presentation so that you can go back and review it if you get stuck on any given point. You will want to refer to it later to make sure the presentation meets the objective and you will also need it for doing practice.

Once you have your basic product presentation, it can be modified for other presenters and other audiences, but it is important to have a target audience and a target objective when building the initial presentation. Failure to do so can result in a presentation that doesn't speak to the audience and one that is not focused on their needs.

Outline of the Product Presentation

(1) Introduction—The speaker introduces themselves, and the main points covered by the product presentation. This is where you want to attract your audience and tell them what is in it for them. (1—2 slides)

(2) Agenda—An agenda is optional, but provides you with an opportunity to tell your audience what you are going to cover in your presentation. It avoids people asking questions early in the presentation about material you will be covering later. (1 slide)

(3) Company Information—This is a way to establish credibility and to make the audience feel comfortable with your company. Ways to do this include customer lists, high-profile executives or advisors, information on funding (if a private company), awards and major milestones.

(4) Positioning—Successful products have a unique technology or positioning that sets them apart from other products on the market. You are supposed to introduce this aspect of your product so as to let your audience know how your product is different and why they should listen to the rest of your presentation. Use this as an attention getter.

(5) Product description—Clearly describe your product in terms that your audience will understand. It may be helpful to have a chart showing the product's components. You want to give the audience a frame of reference for the features and benefits that they are going to see. Show how the product interfaces [connect] with other products or systems they may be using.

(6) Clearly articulated benefits as they relate to your target audience—You can use a features-and-benefits list or just walk through the features and benefits. Whatever you do, do not forget the benefits! (1—5 slides)

(7) Examples/successes—At this point in the presentation your audience should be familiar with your product and why it is different and/or better than other similar products in the market. In order to drive this point home, use examples of how your product is being used and how customers have benefited or will benefit from the product.

(8) Closing argument—This is your opportunity for a "call to action." You should summarize your presentation, reiterate the point of the presentation, and ask your audience to do something, if that is the point of your presentation.

◎ Useful Expressions

present your product in the best light possible

...is different depending upon the target audience and the presentation should be adjusted accordingly

There are also times when...

present this in terms of your audience and their pain

give the audience a frame of reference for ...

live and breathe the product

failure to do so can result in ...

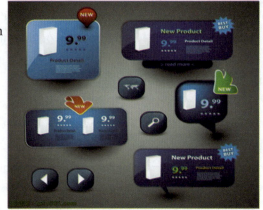

III. Strategies of Product Introduction

New Product Introduction Strategies
By Lee Morgan

Introducing a new product to the market can be a challenging task for a business. No matter how much confidence you have in the value of the product or how unique it is, there are still things to consider before unleashing it on the public. Develop a complete strategy for introducing your new product before putting it on the market.

Know the Target Demographic

Define your target audience. A good product is a good product only if someone wants it. Odds are, as a product developer, you have put some thought into why someone would want to buy the new item. Now decide who, specifically, will want it.

Defining a target demographic is key in successfully launching a new product. Know who will be most likely to buy the product and where they are most likely to look for it. If the new product is a $5,000 designer watch, then a family department store in a financially strapped part of town shouldn't be your venue of choice. Find out who wants to sell it, and work directly with the retailer to brainstorm on how to make the product best appeal to its target audience.

Determine Distribution Methods

Determine how to best distribute the product to make it the most profitable. Maybe consumers should be buying this new product off the shelf at the grocery store, or perhaps direct shipping to the home through online orders make the most sense. It all depends on the target consumer and the product itself.

In some instances the product's primary consumer is the wholesaler. For example, assume the new product is a food item that a wholesaler will sell directly to restaurants. In this event, the distribution is by the wholesale company and you should work directly with the wholesale sales team to instruct them on the best way to present the product to clients and increase their sales, thereby increasing your own.

Immediate Sales Incentives

Offer sales incentives to staff if you are a retail outlet launching an exclusive new product sold only in your stores. With many products competing for consumers' attention, you don't need the additional concern of a new product being ignored by the sales team. An incentive program for the salespeople will keep the new product on their minds and give the launch of a new item the much-needed push to get it off to a successful start quickly.

Internal Launch First

Launch the new product to your own people first. An internal launch will build excitement among the staff about the new product and it will help them to understand its importance. Involving those on the inside with the process of unveiling a new product will likely spill over to the consumer public when the item is released.

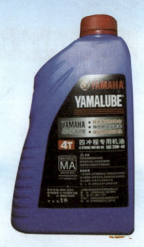

Advertise, Advertise, Advertise

Build anticipation and desire for the product before it is available and after the introduction takes place. This requires advertising. Depending on the product and the anticipated demand from the public, carefully selected target advertising may be adequate. However, a new product that is likely to appeal to the masses may require a massive campaign to saturate the market with the new product information.

IV. Practicing

1. Match the English words and phrases with the proper Chinese meanings.

(1) meet the objective   a. 结构合理
(2) product component   b. 达到目标
(3) rational construction   c. 品种繁多
(4) attractive design   d. 久负盛名
(5) wide varieties   e. 操作简便
(6) dependable performance   f. 规格齐全
(7) easy and simple to handle   g. 深受欢迎
(8) to win warm praise from customers   h. 性能可靠
(9) complete in specifications   i. 款式新颖
(10) have a long standing reputation   j. 产品构件,产品组件

2. Translate the following Chinese sentences into English.

(1) 让我来说明是什么原因使我们的产品销售得那么好。
(2) 我们的产品价格低廉,具有竞争力。
(3) 这种产品的真正优点就是质量高和体积小。
(4) 我们的实验表明这种样式至少可以使用四年。
(5) 在我们这的市场上这款玩具有非常稳固的需求。

Unit 2 Product Introduction

3. Work in pairs and have a conversation.

   You represent China National Electronics Imp & Exp Corp., South China Branch. One of your latest products of this year is called "Sleep Help." It looks like a radio, but it can simulate different kinds of sounds, like those of wind, rainfall, ocean waves, which will help you to sleep. It can also simulate the singing of birds in the morning to wake you up. A businessperson from South Korea who read your advertisement in *China Daily* is quite interested in your product. You should take the opportunity to introduce your product to him. Your introduction should cover the following points: the name of the product, its functions, its quality, its features and the prices.

4. Introduce one of your favorite products.

V. Optional Reading

Other Important Points for Creating a Product Presentation

Use Examples

Use examples whenever possible. Examples help to illustrate your points and provide a frame of reference for those people in your audience that don't already have one.

Simplify

Keep slides as simple as possible. Lots of text on a slide makes it difficult to read and it loses its impact. Make sure the slides will be readable from the back of the room. If you are not giving the presentation, you may feel compelled to add more text to the slides—provide speaker's notes instead.

If you are using PowerPoint, don't get carried away with colors and many different transitions. Pick a format and stick with it so that you don't draw attention away from your subject.

One of the most effective presentations that I ever saw was done with a single clip art picture in the middle of each slide. The picture makes a point without drawing attention away from the speaker.

Easy-to-Read Fonts

A san-serif font (a font that does not have the little lines at the top and bottom, as in the headings of this document) is easier to read for bullets on slides.

Style

A presentation that uses the default PowerPoint fonts and lots of different primary colors looks like a presentation that was slapped together with little thought. Not everyone is a graphic artist, but you can learn some basic principles and apply them to your slides. Below are a few key points, but be sure to read Robin William's *The Non-Designer's Design Book* for more tips.

Use a presentation template and then use the colors from it (or ones in the same family) for all charts and graphs.

Use alignment carefully. If your template is left or right aligned, use that alignment throughout the presentation.

Remove harsh lines. PowerPoint always puts a dark line around any box that you draw. These lines make the drawings look crude and harsh. By removing the lines your eye focuses more on the content of the box rather than the boxes themselves. Additional lines and arrows don't have to be dark either, try making them thicker and lighter so that they don't draw attention away from the point of the slide.

Provide Speaker's Notes

In order to keep the bullets on your slides concise, you may want to consider providing speaker notes to people that may be giving your presentation. If you do provide speaker's notes, keep them short and concise and use bullets to make it easy to read. Remember that the more text you put on the speaker's notes, the less likely the speaker is to read it before the presentation. I can't tell you how many times I have seen a presentation where the speaker says, "I think this slide is trying to say..." Both the speaker and the marketing group that provides the presentation look bad.

If you are using PowerPoint, print the slides with the speaker's notes so that the presenter does not get the notes out of sync with the presentation.

Provide Handouts

You will probably handout copies of the slides. It is always nice to print the slides in a format where there is room for the audience to take notes.

Unit 2 Product Introduction

You may want to use handouts in addition to providing copies of the slides. Often, to keep slides simple, you may compromise the ability for the viewer to use it as a reference later or you may have charts or back-up information that has too much detail to include in your presentation. In these cases it may help to include handouts and refer to them during your presentation.

Use Themes for Group Presentations

If there are a group of people presenting, it is helpful to use a theme and weave it throughout all the presentations. This provides a sense of cohesiveness to the entire presentation.

A good agenda is an important part of group presentations. You want to introduce all the speakers and let the audience know the topic each speaker will be discussing.

Mark Confidential

If the presentation is confidential, don't forget to mark it confidential. Slides often get copied at customer sites and can easily end up in your competitors' hands.

When You are the Presenter

Practice your presentation. No one ever has the time to do it, but even if you are used to winging presentations, the following are the benefits of practice:

1) Your pitch will be more powerful, polished, and professional
2) You are more likely to accomplish your objective
3) You look better

There is nothing worse than watching a presenter bring up a slide and then try to interpret it as if this is the first time they are seeing it. The slides are to support your presentation. I will often give the presentation to a practice audience within the company first before giving it to an external audience. You will get some great suggestions from people who have a slightly different perspective. This is especially true if you can give your pitch to a different department. I have found that giving a product presentation to the engineering group will provide some great insights. Before you give your presentation to a practice audience, be sure to go over the "Points to Consider" above with your audience so that they understand your objective, target audience, and that target audience's perspective.

Additionally you should add slides that talk specifically to your audience. Identify the issues and problems that they are dealing with or tell them about how their competition is doing something. Then show them how your product will provide them with a competitive advantage.

Other Helpful Hints:

Use gestures to make things visual and clear.

Use an expressive voice to emphasize points and show your enthusiasm for your product.

Always stand, even when you are talking to a small audience. Standing projects more energy.

Use highlights or colors on charts to emphasize an important point. (Though don't overuse this, and don't use red unless you want to set off alarms.)

Use controversy — It is sometimes useful to start your presentation with a controversial statement to grab your audience's attention.

Use metaphors to help with visualization.

Make sure you have a smooth verbal transition between slides for a very polished presentation. (This is where the practice really pays off.)

Unit 3 Marketing

Unit Aims

- To gain the basic knowledge about marketing
- To know the difference between marketing, advertising and sales
- To master the basic expressions about marketing

Warming Up

- What is marketing according to your understanding?
- How much do you know about advertising and promotion?
- Consult the Internet for more information about the following social media properties: *Facebook, Twitter, LinkedIn, Myspace, YouTube, Instagram.*

I. Marketing Survey and Target Audience

Dialogue 1

A: I went over the sales figures in the market research report. If you take that report and compare it with our survey of consumer buying habits, there's only one conclusion.

B: What's that?

A: It seems this market is sensitive to price. When our product was marked up at a higher introductory price, our sales after product launch were lower than low. At a discounted introductory price, we landed more sales.

B: So, we should start low?

A: I think that would be a good idea. Price is an important variable in our market, so we can use it to build our customer base. If our customers get hooked on the low introductory price, they will buy and become more loyal to our brand. Later on, when we hit a peak in sales and after our customer base is sold on our products, we can bring the price up.

B: That sounds like a really clever marketing strategy.

A: This is a very competitive market. We've got to come up with a few clever strategies in order to keep our place on top.

B: I think our main strength is with young consumers.

A: That's who we are targeting. The young consumer is fast to commit, but fickle to stay with a brand. Our challenge is customer loyalty.

Dialogue 2

A: What's our target audience for this campaign?

B: This go-around we're focusing on new moms, families with median income and one or more children under the age of two.

A: Do you think that's much different from the soccer moms we tailored the last campaign for?

B: Well, there are some similarities that come up. Because both groups are made up of mothers, so as before, we can play up on maternal instincts, hygiene, safety, along those lines. But that being said, there are some specific differences that come into play because we are dealing with mothers of infants here.

A: Right, that makes sense. What's the average age?

B: Demographics say in average age of 28.7, educational back ground of university or post-grad, annual household income of 40—50K a year.

◎ Useful Expressions

Marketing research is broader and involves more functions of sales.
The preliminary market test is due to start next month.
Our sales reached the target and the customers' reaction was good.
They have no problems with production during the test market phase.
Our turnover last year was $650,000.
Our sales were up twelve percent last year.
What's your market share?

Unit 3　Marketing

II. Market Strategy, Advertising and Promotion

Dialogue 1

In this conversation, Tanya Nichols, the owner of an ice-cream manufacturing company, is talking with her marketing manager, Carla Hutchison, about the marketing strategy for a new product.

Tanya:　So, Carla, do you have a marketing plan for our new ice-cream sandwich?

Carla:　Yes, I do. After going through our S.W.O.T. process, I think we're in good shape. One of our main strengths is the quality of our ice-cream, and there's a good market opportunity for the novelty of a choice of flavors. Since our company already has a good image, I don't see many weaknesses. No other company sells ice-cream sandwiches with a choice of 5 flavors, so there's no threat to speak of, either.

Tanya:　I assume we don't need to worry about creating a need, with summer almost here.

Carla:　Right. As for the marketing mix, we'll package it in gold foil with dark brown lettering to simulate chocolate, and price it 20% higher than our chocolate-covered ice-cream bar. It'll be introduced in selected places across the country starting next month. The main promotion will be through advertising, using a "pull" strategy, of course. We haven't finalized our ads yet, so I'll have to let you know. Can we meet again the beginning of next week?

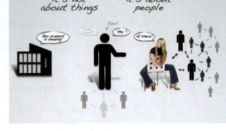

Tanya:　Sure can. Let me check ... how about Tuesday morning at 10:30?

Carla:　Uh, let's see ... okay with me.

Dialogue 2

Tanya:　Good morning, Carla. How are you today?

Carla:　I'm doing fine. How about you?

Tanya:　Great, thanks. So, what's the status of our advertising campaign?

Carla:　As I mentioned before, a national campaign will start next month. We've decided to use a variety of media for full coverage. First, we'll have 30-second spots on television once a day for 3 weeks. At the same time, we'll do 15-second radio commercials 3 times a day in selected cities with large populations. Finally, we'll have some outdoor ads using billboards near the main entrances to big cities.

Tanya:　What will the ads be?

Carla:　We're focusing on slice of life, showing how you can beat the summer heat by biting into a cool ice-cream sandwich. We'll also show everyone there are variety of flavors and they're not stuck with just vanilla.

Tanya: Sounds like an ideal approach. Will we have a new slogan?

Carla: Definitely. The advertising agency's working on that right now. They'll have some proposals ready by the end of the week.

Tanya: Sounds like we'll have a winner on our hands!

Dialogue 3

A: Market classifieds, how may I help you?

B: Yes, I would like to find out about placing an advertisement in your directory. Can you tell me a little about your rates for advertisements?

A: Certainly. Our advertising rates are divided according to size, substrate, and location. If you are a corporate partner with our publication, we can offer you a slight discount. Also, our rates are different according to which publication you wish to advertise in. Our fall edition is pricier than the spring edition. When were you looking to advertise?

B: We would like to get in with the fall publication if possible.

A: We can do that, timing might be a little tight because our press day is October 25th, but it can be done. Do you have a pre-determined design? You can use either your own designers or if it is more than convenient for you, we have a team of inhouse graphic designers that can put something together for you.

B: That won't be necessary, we already have the image. If we run a full page ad in your fall edition on a normal gloss paper, tri-color, what do you think that will run me?

A: It depends on the location in the material. Are you interested in the front or back page ad? Those were prime spots. We also have 6 tab page positions available.

B: I think a tab spot would be nice.

A: For a customer supplied design, full page tab page ad. You're looking at about 785 dollars.

Dialogue 4

M: What kind of promotional events are scheduled for the new product line?

F: Marketing has us set up with product launches in five major cities, as well as some sponsoring events throughout the year. Altogether, there will be 15 events.

M: What kind of sponsoring are we talking about? I don't know how effective sponsorship really is...

F: It's not what you're thinking. These events will give us a wider exposure than most. Take the tri-city marathon for starters. This is a highly publicized event. The television exposure alone will nearly double our customer awareness.

M: Other than the marathon, what else is on the list?

F: We've got a spot in Olympic Stadium sponsoring one of a team's equipment, then a rally for cancer research, and a connection to the inner-city education program.

M: Sports, medicine, education... seems kind of random, don't you think?

F: It might seem that way, but these events were all carefully chosen based on marketing research. These are the events that our customers and potential customers care about.

◎ **Useful Expressions**

buying habit	购买习惯
product launch	产品发布
variable	变量,变数
get hooked on sth.	上钩;被某事迷住了
stay with a brand	忠于一个品牌
go-around	回合

package it in gold foil with dark brown lettering to simulate chocolate 用像巧克力一样的深褐色字母的金箔纸来包装它

tab page	标签页
Soccer moms	(子女爱看足球的)足球妈妈
tailor	专门制作,定做

Sometimes a company tries to build its corporate image through advertising.
The social and cultural aspects must be taken into account in advertising, too.
We usually make different commercials for each market.
Electric advertising is quick, cheap and widespread.
Haier Group makes its brand quite famous among children through cartoons.
I think your letter pretty well covered it.
I just follow up and make sure you got my letter last week.
Is there a demand for your product/service?
There is a poor market for these articles.
There is no market for these articles.
Please furnish us with more information from time to time so that we may find outlets for our stationery.
They are doing their utmost to open up an outlet.
We are sure that you can sell more this year according to the marketing conditions at your end.
According to our experience, these ... can find a ready market in...

We can discuss further details when you have a thorough knowledge of the marketing possibilities of our products.

The market situation is not known to us.

According to your estimate, what is the maximum annual turnover you could fulfill? Your market still has great potential.

There are only a few unsold pieces.

Thanks for all the work you've done to promote the sale of our products.

This diagram shows ...(total net income)

We have...(the right product ranges for today's market place)

Thanks for all the work you've done to promote the sale of our products.

The market responds well to...

Price depends. We may consider volume discount.

If quantity is large, some variety can also proper favorable.

If you want large quantities, we will give you lower prices.

I hope our products will be to your customers' liking.

This is the most powerful engine in its class.

Is your product suitable for the advertising specialty or premium market?

We are having a promotion this week.

We have pleasure in recommending to you the following goods.

You are so lucky. They are on sale today. It costs only 180 *yuan*.

III. Marketing

What Is Marketing?

What is marketing? It is a question that people who do not work in the discipline sometimes ask (or perhaps should ask).

The idea of marketing

Once upon a time, in the age of barter, people made stuff that they needed and swapped spares with others to get other things they needed. Although the word "marketing" was a long way off, they still had to tell people about what they had available and be careful about their reputation. Marketing has always existed. Only recently has it become a formal discipline.

The basic idea of marketing is that it is not enough just to make what you think will sell and then put it in the shop window in the hope of passers-by seeing it and wanting it. If you do this, you may sell a few but it will also mean:

- Many people will not know that the product exists.
- Those who see it may not know what it is or what it is for.
- Those who understand it may not appreciate how it can help them.
- Those who want it may not be willing to pay what you are asking (or actually think it's a real bargain but keep quiet about this).
- The product may actually be of little real value to anyone.

When merchants started selling other people's goods, the need to tell people about the goods increased with the size of their market and the novelty of the goods. As the industrial revolution progressed and markets expanded, the need for marketing increased further.

Marketing as a broad professional discipline only really took off in the latter half of the 20th century, even though principles such as advertising had been used for many years beforehand.

Definition

The American Marketing Association defines marketing as:

The activity, set of institutions, and processes for creating, communicating, delivering, and exchanging offerings that have value for customers, clients, partners, and society at large.

As with many institutions, the definition of their domain is somewhat all-encompassing and consequently rather vague.

A dictionary definition is more precise, although this would make many marketers shriek as it includes sales but excludes earlier activities such as market research and specification of the product or service:

The process of promoting, selling, and distributing a product or service.

In his classic textbook, Kotler (1996) defines marketing with a more distinct concern for customers in a view that highlights an equitable value exchange (which is reminiscent of ancient barter) rather than the more traditional marketing push:

A social and managerial process by which individuals and groups obtain what they need and want through creating and exchanging products and value with others.

A simpler yet wide definition frames marketing as facilitating the difficult space between creation and consumption of products. This includes both pushing new products and developing products that are needed:

Matching supply and demand.

The word "marketing" is also used as an abbreviation for "the marketing department," being those people whose profession is marketing.

Discussion

Marketing can be broken down in various ways. The simplest is to break it into two distinct areas: inbound marketing, which is about researching customers and shaping product designs, and outbound marketing, which is mostly about traditional product promotion.

It is noteworthy that marketing is an active verb without any implied activity completion. This may be contrasted with "sales" and "development." It perhaps reflects the difficulty of the job, as it is not easy to know when you have succeeded. Even if the product sells well, then the Development and Sales people will likely say it was their efforts that made the real difference.

Retail and business marketing are similar, but different. Business buyers are professional and usually know more of what they want, although increasingly retail customers are also surprisingly well informed.

Is marketing just "helping sellers sell"? As Kotler (1996) points out, it's an exchange, so it should also be involved in helping buyers buy. Pushing products blindly can be counter-productive as pressure methods destroy trust, which is a key gateway if you seek credibility. This makes marketing a difficult balancing act and sometimes neutral trust agents need to be employed in some way.

Marketing often includes brand management (although brand managers may well reverse this order) and is concerned with how all aspects of the product and the organisation align in creating a consistent product and customer experience.

The difference between marketing and sales is also often unclear, although broadly sales people go out and find specific customers then persuade them to make actual purchases. This is often done using information and material from the marketing people. Marketing done well creates demand that makes selling much easier.

Marketers may also work all the way up and down the supply chain, marketing to and working with suppliers, resellers and others to ensure a consistency of product and service.

IV. Practicing

1. Match the English words and phrases with the proper Chinese meanings.

(1) selling line   a. 战略营销

(2) trial sale, test sale, test market   b. 销路

(3) salable goods   c. 热门货

(4) the best-selling line (the best seller)   d. 顾客满意度

(5) to have a strong footing in a market   e. 畅销,销得很快

(6) sell like wild fire   f. 经销渠道

(7) controllable components   g. 畅销货

(8) sales record   h. 销售记录

Unit 3 Marketing

(9) customers' satisfaction　　　　i. 可控因素
(10) facilitating agent　　　　　　 j. 试销
(11) distribution channel　　　　　k. 服务代理商
(12) marketing objective　　　　　 l. 很有销路
(13) strategic marketing　　　　　 m. 目标市场
(14) target market　　　　　　　　 n. 销售业绩
(15) potential threats and opportunities　o. 营销目标
(16) sales performance　　　　　　 p. 潜在的风险和机遇

2. Fill in the blanks with the following words and phrases.

market share	breakdown	retail
distribute	run through	at your leisure
commission	in stock	at long last
target	synchronize	sector
in terms of	market penetration	
market demand		

(1) The computer company was forced to reduce prices to keep its _____.
(2) The _____ for a product is affected by its price.
(3) Please give me a _____ of those income tax totals by age groups.
(4) We will _____ our campaign at young home-buyers.
(5) As I was in haste to leave for a meeting yesterday, I just _____ this list of figures and didn't notice it.
(6) _____ we found out what really happened to our last delivery.
(7) The launch date for this new product is the first of May 2006 and will then _____ to our main retail outlets.
(8) Mr Brown _____ to set up a branch in London.
(9) Please fill in the form _____ and post it to us.
(10) If you have fountain pens _____, please send us some samples.
(11) They referred to your service _____ high praise.
(12) We have changed our packaging to appeal to all age groups in order to obtain maximum _____.
(13) These items _____ at £5.99.
(14) The closing of the old store _____ with the opening of the new shopping plaza.
(15) The agricultural _____ in western nations is highly subsidized.

3. Translate the following Chinese sentences into English.

(1) 现在我们已经决定走全球化路线。我们应该采取什么形式进入美国市场?

(2) 但是他们关于本地市场的知识可能会大有价值。

(3) 我们相信对于能在居民市场上开辟出新行业的公司来说这种新产品为他们带来莫大的市场机遇。

(4) 我们可以在那边设一个办事处。它可以通过外面的营销代理公司组织营销和销售活动。

(5) 几个月后我还会向大家报告促销活动的细节。

V. Optional Reading

Market Players

There are often a number of different types of companies or people playing in any marketplace.

Customers

Of course the most important organization or people in the market are your customers. This includes both current and potential customers.

Major customers

It is very common for most sales to be made to a relatively small set of big customers. These always need careful attention and may have account/relationship managers assigned to them. A problem is that big customers may also demand big discounts and special attention.

Minor customers

Minor customers buy less, but nevertheless are useful as in aggregate they may buy quite a lot. The only time minor customers are undesirable is when serving them costs more than the profit gained from them. This can happen when they are angered or when they try to gain an unfair attention for their smaller payment.

Suppliers

Suppliers may sell directly into the market, for example selling spare parts, but largely they need to be kept aligned to your strategy.

In some markets suppliers also supply your competitors. When supply is short, the supplier may hold a position of power in the choice of who to serve.

You can also have major and minor suppliers. Major suppliers are critical for everyday delivery and a problem from them can cause delays or product quality issues.

Complementors

Complementors are those who sell non-competing products and which generally help your sales. For example in a rock musical instrument market, drum and guitar manufacturers are complementors to one another.

It is generally a good idea to collaborate closely with complementors as mutual benefit may be gained. They may also seek to work with competitors, which can be a tricky situation—but if it all adds up to expanding the market, then this is beneficial. An alternative strategy, as with suppliers, is that if you can lead the complementors to support you more, then competitors may be weakened.

Competitors

Competitors are those who have products and services similar to you and where customers who are buying something will compare your offerings and prices directly, weighing one up against the other.

The interaction with competitors is usually directly antagonistic. You seek to convince customers that your offerings are better and that competitors' offerings are worse. Nevertheless, there are times when collaborating with competitors is helpful, for example in influencing sensible regulations.

Substitutors

Substitutors are like competitors but their products are not the same. The classic substitution is replacing butter with margarine (a battle that is still raging). Other substitutions are more evolutionary, for example where typewriters were substituted by wordprocessors.

Initially, substitutions may be seen as quite different, for example where computers were big and expensive alternatives to the typewriter. Yet innovation and evolution continued and computers eventually became cheaper than typewriters as well as offering benefits the typewriter could not emulate.

A critical attribute of a substitutor group is that they all seek the same "share of wallet." Hence, when a person is thirsty, all drinks are substitutes for one another.

Regulators

In any industry, standards are often helpful in many ways, from ensuring product safety to helping suppliers create plug-compatible parts that enable economies of scale and hence lower product prices.

Regulation may be driven by collaboration between competitors. Regulations may also be created by independent organizations or even governments, whose agendas may not align with company profit motives.

An important part of regulation is policing, without which regulations become only guidelines. Sometimes customers do their own policing, for example by not buying non-standard products. Regulation may also be done by independent inspectors who can have draconian punitive powers.

It can be an important part of marketing to demonstrate conformance to regulations. Displaying safety badges, showing ecological awards, and so on can help convince customers of the quality of the product and the integrity of the firm.

Influencers

There are also groups and organizations who have no direct control but who will seek to promote their own agendas by influencing players within the marketplace, including regulators and retailers. These often have an ethical basis, for example ecological or animal rights activists.

Lobby groups who represent certain business interests may also be involved, although often indirectly (for example in seeking to persuade regulators to create stronger controls).

Marketers need to be careful with influencers who can create bad publicity through demonstrations and leaking information to the press. Influencers can be helpful if you listen to them and take their concerns seriously.

Unit 4 Purchase Order

Unit Aims

- To master purchase order conditions
- To know how a case is accomplished in the international trade
- To know how to create a purchase order

Warming Up

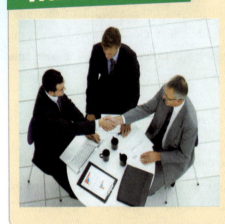

An overseas buyer, Mr. Wise is inclined to issue a purchase order to Shanghai Import and Export Corporation. Mr. Joe is the manager of the corporation with Miss Li as his secretary. Miss Li is preparing some sentences for the negotiation. What other sentences can you add to the list?

When can we discuss the contract?

We would like to discuss the means of delivery in detail.

There are some points we have not worked out.

I. Place a Purchase Order

Joe: Good morning, Mr. Wise. You have had a good trip, haven't you?

Wise: Yes. A very good journey, thank you. We've had your offer and are very much interested in it.

Joe: I wonder if you have found that our specification meet your requirements. I'm sure the prices we submitted are competitive.

Wise: Oh, yes, and I've come to place an order with you. We like the design of your ivory carvings. My company will send you an official confirmation soon. But there are a few

	questions sought to be settled. For example, the cost for sending the goods.
Joe:	Yes, I see. We quoted you as warehouse price. If you want me to give you the price FOB, that would cover the transport from our house to deck and all the handling and shipping charges that will include wharfage, porterage, buck dues and port rates, leaving to pay the sea freights and marine insurance. Is that what you want?
Wise:	No. I think we should prefer to have an idea of the total costs delivering right to our port.
Joe:	Then what about a CIF price? That would cover the cost of the goods; a comprehensive insurance with a clause from warehouse to warehouse; all the forwarding and shipping charges and fees paid to your port.
Wise:	But there will be a few things left for us to pay.
Joe:	Yes, the charges for your forward agent for clearing the goods, paying custom duties and arranging delivery to your sight. I can get the CIF prices worked out by our shipping department when we go on talking. Miss Li, take this price quotation to the shipping department and get them to work out CIF prices for Mr. Wise, will you?
Wise:	I would like to ask you next, Mr. Joe, about delivery. How soon can it be effected?
Joe:	We will take partial deliveries. I mean, we could let you have, say 1/3 of the order immediately from the stock. And this can be dispatched just as soon as we can get the shipping space. In this case, I suggest you make your order on shipping schedule divided in three, each within interval of 3 weeks.
Wise:	Good.
Joe:	And final consignment would be for forward delivery at a future time when the goods are available from the mills.
Wise:	Excuse me, but we should like to have the definite date for the last shipment.
Joe:	Of course. You can stipulate in your order saying final shipment not later than such a date, some dates on which we could agree which could be met by the mill's supplement.
Wise:	Good. That is the best I know they can do.
Joe:	That depends on their production program and the orders they have on the books. I should inquire, not about yourself, you are not pressed for time, aren't you?
Wise:	Oh, no.
Joe:	Good, well. While Miss Li is typing out this quotation, perhaps you'll have something to drink with me.
Wise:	Thank you very much. I should like to.

◎ Useful Expressions

◎ When talking about inquiries and replies you may hear:

We are interested in your company. We would greatly appreciate receiving any information, brochures and price lists you may have to learn more about your products.

We are enclosing our catalog and price list for your review and are confident that this literature will provide many of the answers you have requested.

If there is additional information you would like to have regarding our products, please do not hesitate to contact us. We will be most happy to be of assistance.

I believe you have seen our exhibits in our show room. What is that particularly you're interested in?

Would you tell us what quantity you require so that we can work out the offer?

We regret that the goods you inquire about are not available.

◎ When talking about prices you may hear:

May I have an idea of your prices?

Could you give me an indication of the price?

Would you tell us your best prices C.I.F. Hamberg for the chairs.

Will you please tell the quantity you require so as to enable us to sort out the offers?

Your price is inacceptable (unacceptable) / feasible (infeasible) / reasonable (unreasonable) / practicable (impracticable) / attractive (not attractive) / inducing (not inducing) / competitive (not competitive).

Price is rising (falling) / looking up.

Price has skyrocketed/risen perpendicularly.

Price is easy off.

Price has declined/plummeted/downslided/dipped.

Since the prices of the raw materials have been raised, I'm afraid that we have to adjust the prices of our products accordingly.

Articles of everyday use are economically priced.

I can give you a definite answer on the price terms.

◎ When talking about quality and quantity you may hear:

If the quality of your products is satisfactory, we may place regular orders.

There is no marked qualitative difference between the two.

We sincerely hope the quality is in conformity with the contract stipulations.

Let's talk about the problem of quantity.

You'll issue a certificate of quantity and weight.

The package number and quantity are identical with each other.

best/superior/good/high/fine/fair/standard/common quality

above/below the average quality

fair average quality

◎ When talking about payment you may hear:

Shall we have a talk about terms of payment today?

What is the mode of payment you wish to employ?

This is the normal terms of payment in international business.

We can't accept any other terms of payment.

Please protect our draft on presentation

Your draft will be honoured on presentation.

◎ When talking about insurance you may hear:

After loading the goods on board the hip, I go to the insurance company to have them insured.

What risks should be covered?

What kind of insurance are you able to provide for my consignment?

It's better for you to scan the leaflet, and then make a decision.

May I ask what exactly insurance covers according to your usual C.I.F terms?

◎ When talking about shipment you may hear:

Can our order of 100 cars be shipped as soon as possible?

Could you possibly effect shipment more promptly?

Could you do something to advance your shipment?

The cargo has been shipped on board S.S. "Dong Feng."

We can get preferential duty rates when we ship to the U.S.A.

The shipment has arrived in good condition.

II. How to Create a Purchase Order

A purchase order is a necessity for just about any company that sells products or needs to order parts and materials. The purchase order tells a vendor exactly what the purchaser needs, and the date the purchaser needs the product in hand. It's simple to draw up a purchase order template that you can use in your day-to-day operations.

Step 1

Employ a standard word processing program to create your purchase order.

Step 2

Add your business name, address, phone number, fax number, email address and additional identifying information at the very top of your purchase order, just as you would list the information in a standard business letter. Provide a receiving address if it's different from your main business address, so that the vendor will send the product to the right place.

Unit 4 Purchase Order

Step 3

Type in the vendor's contact information, including his business name, address and phone number. List a purchase order number and the date, as well as the payment remittance or Bill-to address, if it's different from your main business address, next to the vendor's information.

Step 4

List a description of the items that you want to order from the vendor. Include the name, item number, quantity, and extended price of the item—the wholesale rate that you and the vendor have agreed upon. This way, if there is any confusion about the price, the vendor can contact you with the correct price before fulfilling your order. This also will avoid disagreements later.

Step 5

Create a subtotal line on which you list the total price before applicable taxes, a tax line for sales tax due and a total line on which you list the total amount due to the vendor for this purchase order.

Step 6

Provide a deadline date for the vendor to fill the purchase order. You need to include this date to avoid receiving the product after you no longer need it. List any additional terms associated with the order, such as the number of days you have to pay your invoice, and who is responsible for paying for the freight. If the vendor pays freight, you can simply type in FOB (free on board).

Step 7

Ask the vendor to note in the shipment if any of the items are on back order or no longer available, so that you can update your records. You can add this and other special instructions to a separate Memo area at the bottom of the purchase order.

Step 8

Sign the bottom of each purchase order, so that your vendor will know that it's authorized by your company.

Tips

- If you are ordering wholesale for the first time from the vendor, you may have to provide a copy of your seller's permit, issued by your state, and pay for your product upfront until you establish a credit history with the vendor.
- If you require a tax identification number from the vendor to issue payment, request that in the "Memo" area.

◎ Tips: A sample purchase order is given below

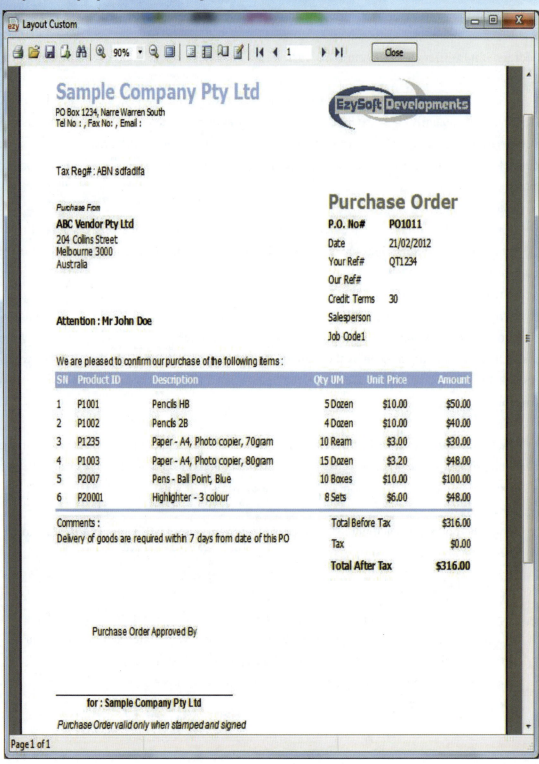

III. Purchase Order Conditions

A purchase order (PO) is a commercial document issued by a buyer to a seller, indicating types, quantities, and agreed prices for products or services the seller will provide to the buyer. Sending a purchase order to a supplier constitutes a legal offer to buy products or services. Acceptance of a purchase order by a seller usually forms a contract between the buyer and seller, so no contract exists until the purchase order is accepted. It is used to control the purchasing of products and services from external suppliers.

Since a purchase order is a legal agreement between a buyer and a seller, it is important that the conditions of the order are laid out clearly and precisely in order to prevent any disagreements between the two parties. Common purchase order conditions include cost, description of materials, date expected, and freight obligations.

One of the most important of the purchase order conditions is the cost of the item, which shows how much the buyer is willing to pay for the goods or services. If the recipient of the purchase order cannot or will not match the cost on the purchase order, he or she must indicate so to the buyer. If the seller proceeds with the order, he or she is obligated to sell the product to the buyer at the price indicated on the purchase order.

A good purchase order has a description of materials which leaves no element of doubt. The issuer of a purchase order should be as specific as possible in order to avoid any confusion later. Expected goods or services must be described with as much detail as possible within the body of the purchase order.

Turn-around time is another of the purchase order conditions. Large manufacturers, or even small manufacturers with just-in-time inventory, often require long lead times in order to process an order. If a seller cannot meet a specified deadline, he or she must indicate so to the buyer and not accept the order unless the deadline time is negotiable.

Freight On Board (FOB) is a popular condition of purchase orders. This indicates who takes responsibility for the cost of the freight, and from what location. If a buyer in New York City purchases a truckload of rugs from San Francisco, the terms might be "FOB New York City" which means that the seller must pay for the freight to get to New York City. If the terms are "FOB San Francisco," this means that the buyer is responsible for the cost of transit. Freight terms are particularly tricky when dealing with international shipping, and the buyer and seller must both be clear on who is paying customs duties and taxes as well as for the actual freight transit.

Standard payment terms in the US are "Net 30," which means that an invoice must be paid within 30 days. Other standard terms are "Net 15." "Net 60," "Net 90" or "Due Upon Receipt." If a purchase order is paid with a credit card, there is usually no need for payment terms to be designated, but there should be clarification on when the credit card is processed for the order.

Purchase order conditions are negotiable most of the time. With a little give and take on the parts of both the buyer and seller, the terms of an order can be modified to appease either party. Some purchase order conditions are non-negotiable, and the buyer or seller should indicate that at the start of negotiation.

◎ **Useful Expressions**

◎ *When talking about inquiries and replies you may hear:*

We are interested in your company. We would greatly appreciate receiving any information, brochures and price lists you may have to learn more about your products.

We are enclosing our catalog and price list for your review and are confident that this literature will provide many of the answers you have requested.

If there is additional information you would like to have regarding our products, please do not hesitate to contact us. We will be most happy to be of assistance.

I believe you have seen our exhibits in our show room. What is that particularly you're interested in?

Would you tell us what quantity you require so that we can work out the offer?

We regret that the goods you inquire about are not available.

◎ *When sending an inquiry letter you may write in this way:*

[Date]
[NAME, COMPANY AND ADDRESS, ex.
Tom Atkinson
COMANY Inc.
14 Edith Street,
Hackney West,
ZIP POST CODE]
Dear [NAME, ex. Tom Atkinson],

　　We are interested in [PRODUCT(S), ex. lubrication materials for A52 compressors used in refrigeration manufacturing]. We would greatly appreciate your providing any information, brochures and price lists you may have to learn more about your products. Please send such materials to:

[ADDRESS, ex.
Attention: Tony Montana
WareSoft Industries
1242A Yonge Street
Toronto, Ontario
L4D 4F2]

I thank you in advance and look forward to studying the materials you send me.

Sincerely,

[YOUR NAME, ex. Tony Montana]

◎ *When making a reply you may write in this way:*

[Date]

[NAME, COMPANY AND ADDRESS, ex.

Tony Montana

WareSoft Industries

1242A Yonge Street

Toronto, Ontario

L4D 4F2]

Dear [NAME, ex. Tony Montana],

  Thank you for your recent inquiry about [nature of inquiry]. We are enclosing our catalog and price list for your review and are confident that this literature will provide many of the answers you have requested.

  If there is additional information you would like to have regarding our products, please do not hesitate to contact us. We will be most happy to be of assistance.

Thank you for the very kind words you used to describe our line of products.

Very truly yours,

[YOUR NAME, ex. Tom Atkinson]

IV. Practicing

1. Match the words and phrases in the left column with the meaning in the right column.

(1) have a good shape   a. in a sound condition
           b. have a good appearance

(2) meet   a. come face to face
          b. satisfy

(3) quote   a. repeat in speech or writing words previously said by another one
          b. name an mount as the price of something

(4) CIF   a. cost, insurance and freight
          b. China International Fund

(5) forward agent   a. a person or company that organizes shipments for individuals or corporations to get goods from the manufacturer to a market
          b. a company suited in front

(6) effect   a. result or outcome
                         b. bring something about

2. **Word families: Complete the following sentences with words related to the key words. (You might need to add prefixes or suffixes and change the form.)**

   identify

   (1) Never give out _____ information such as Name, Home Address, School Name, or Telephone Number in a public message such as at a chat room or on bulletin boards.

   (2) A Tax _____ Number or TIN is an identifying number used for tax purposes in the US. It may be assigned by the SSN or IRS.

   (3) There are a number of distinguishing characteristics by which you can _____ a fake Ipad.

   contact

   (1) If there is additional information you would like to have regarding our products, please do not hesitate to _____ us.

   (2) This may involve _____ the customer for an order modification.

   (3) It can also be done by establishing direct contact with the World Trade Organization.

   fulfill

   (1) We regret that our manufacturers cannot undertake to _____ your order owing to the uncertain availability of raw material.

   (2) In a typical supply chain integration project, for example, marketing, sales, _____, and finance are all stakeholders.

   (3) Have you _____ commitments to yourself and others?

3. **Writing practice**

   Try to finish the following purchase order according to your negotiation in part I.

   [Company Name]
   [Your Company Slogan]

   # PURCHASE ORDER

   [Street Address]
   [City, ST ZIP Code]
   Phone [   ] Fax [   ]

   The following number must appear on all related correspondence, shipping papers, and invoices:
   P.O. NUMBER: [001] (The number assigned to the purchase order)

Unit 4 Purchase Order

VENDOR: (Supplier Name and Address)
[Name]
[Company]
[Street Address]
[City, ST ZIP Code]
[Phone]

SHIP TO: (Receiving Department address of the buyer)
[Name]
[Company]
[Street Address]
[City, ST ZIP Code]
[Phone]

P.O. DATE	REQUISITIONER	SHIPPED VIA	F.O.B. POINT	TERMS
The date the purchase order was originated	The person who requested the order	Shipping instructions entered by Purchasing Department	Shipping terms defined by Purchasing Department	Payment terms defined by Purchasing Department

QTY	UNIT	DESCRIPTION	UNIT PRICE	TOTAL
Quantity of the good or service	The unit of measurement (e.g.,each,box, lot)	Briefly describes the goods or services being required, all relevant information must be provided to ensure appropriate terms and conditions are applied on the Purchase Order.	Requires the price for each unit of measure.	
		SUBTOTAL		
		SALES TAX		
		SHIPPING & OTHER		
		TOTAL		The total amount of all items on the purchase order

Please send two copies of your invoice.

Enter this order in accordance with the prices, terms, delivery method, and specifications listed above.

Please notify us immediately if you are unable to ship as specified.

Send all correspondence to:
  [Name]
  [Street Address]
  [City, ST ZIP Code]

Phone   Fax

_____
Authorized by   Date

V. Optional Reading

Purchase Order Number

Also known simply as a PO number, a purchase order number is an alphanumeric code that is assigned to each order that a business places with a vendor. Internally, the number makes it possible to apply the costs of those orders to the budgets of the departments that placed the orders. The PO number also provides the accounts payable team with verification that the expense is legitimate and payment may be rendered to the vendor.

In many company settings, the purchase order number is assigned after a department submits a request for the order of certain goods and services. The request is formally submitted to a purchasing agent, typically using what is known as a requisition form. If the request is approved, a purchase order is created, and the purchase order number is associated with the requisition. At that point, the order is placed with a vendor, who also records the PO number for inclusion on the order detail.

As the vendor prepares a shipping or packing list to go with the customer's order, the purchase order number is included as a reference on the detail. This makes it possible for the receiving agent at the customer's place of business to not only check the quantity and type of goods delivered, but also to confirm that the shipment is associated with a properly authorized order. In like manner, the purchase order number also appears on the invoice and any other correspondence that the vendor issues to the customer. From this perspective, the PO number expedites the scheduling of payment to the vendor, and also allows the goods to be routed to the proper department with a minimum of delay.

The exact construction of a purchase order number will vary from one company to another. Many businesses that operate multiple locations and make use of a central purchasing department will use the first three or four characters of the number to identify the facility location. The next several characters may have to do with the sequencing of orders placed on behalf of the location, while the remaining characters often help to associate the order with the department within the facility that ultimately receives the items ordered. Companies structure PO numbers in whatever manner works best with their internal tracking systems. In response to this, many vendors configure the fields in their order tracking databases to allow up to thirty characters for the purchase order number.

Unit 5 Finance

Unit Aims

- To get basic knowledge of the American Financial System
- To know how to get Housing Loans
- To know how to open a Savings Account

Warming Up

Suppose you were going to start your business in the U.S., what do you need to get to know about American Financial System? Is there a central bank of the state? What's the function of it? In this part, we are going to focus on American Federal Reserve System, concentrating on its function, authority, ownership, etc.

I. The American Financial System

Iwao Tanaka, making his first business trip to the United States, is talking to an American banker about the financial and monetary system of the U.S.

Tanaka: What is meant by the term Federal Reserve System? Is that the central bank of the United States?

Banker: Technically it is not, Mr. Tanaka, but it functions in that capacity. The Federal Reserve System, or the Fed as it is usually called, is the fiscal agent of the United States. It has authority to issue notes which are the main currency of the country, to control the money supply and to supervise banks and banking practices in the country.

Tanaka: It's owned by the government, isn't it?

Banker: No, it isn't. Actually, the Fed really consists of 12 banks which are owned by all the nationally chartered banks in their respective districts. But the supervisory board, called the Board of Governors, is a government agency responsible to the Congress.

Tanaka: What do you mean by nationally chartered banks? Don't all banks have to have charters?

Banker: Yes, every bank must have a charter or license to do business. But we have a dual banking system here in the United States. That means some banks are licensed by the federal government and some by individual states. There are approximately 5,000 national banks and 10,000 state banks in the country.

Tanaka: Are they all supervised by the Fed?

Banker: Only the national banks are.

Tanaka: I suppose that means that for all practical purposes the Fed controls the state chartered banks, too.

Banker: Yes, I would say that's correct. The Fed has the final authority on controlling the supply of money, and that alone has a great impact on any bank.

Tanaka: You said earlier that the Fed issues the main currency of the country. Do you mean that there are several forms of currency?

Banker: Historically, there have been a number of different issues of currency. Some notes have been issued by the Treasury and some by the Fed. Actually, if you look carefully at the notes you have in your possession, you'll find some that say United States Note, some that say Federal Reserve Bank Note and even some that say National Bank Note. These are all forms of old issues that are gradually being retired from circulation.

Tanaka: Therefore, the Federal Reserve Note is the main one today?

Banker: Yes, that's right. It's what we call flat money or currency without any gold or silver backing. We all accept it as money because the government declares it to be money.

Tanaka: Yes, that's the same as the situation in Japan. I think that's true in all modern nations today.

Banker: Yes, in paper currency as well as coinage. Modern coins are called token money for that reason.

◎ Useful Expressions

fiscal agent	财务代理
Federal Reserve System	联邦储备体系
fiat money	法定货币

commercial bank	商业银行
industrial bank	工业银行
Savings and Loan Association	储蓄与贷款协会
lend money for mortgages	抵押贷款
savings account	储蓄账户
check(ing) account	支票账户
current account	活期存款账户
make loans	放贷

II. Opening a Savings Account

Henry Samson is asking a clerk at the First National Bank about opening a regular savings account.

Clerk: May I help you, sir?

Samson: Yes, please. I'd like to open a savings account. Can you give me some information?

Clerk: Yes, I'd be happy to help you. We call our regular savings account plan passbook savings. You may open an account in your name only, or a joint account with your wife. There is no minimum balance, and you may make deposits or withdrawals at any time.

Samson: Do I earn interest on the account?

Clerk: Yes, we pay the highest interest rate permitted for commercial banks. We credit the earned interest to your account automatically every quarter.

Samson: Is it difficult to open an account? I mean, do I have to be a regular customer of the bank?

Clerk: No, sir, not at all. All that's necessary is to fill out this signature card and make your initial deposit. Even a dollar is enough to open the account.

Samson: Let's see. You want my name, address, occupation, date of birth and Social Security number. What's this item here, "Mother's Maiden Name"?

Clerk: We ask that for identification purposes, sir. It's a code word we use to positively identify you in case you lose your passbook or there is some other need for positive identification.

Samson: I see. Well, let me fill this out and I'll open an account.

Talking about Housing Loans

Al and Virginia Baxter are talking to their banker, Tony Flora, about a housing loan.

Al: We'd like to get some information about mortgage loans, Mr. Flora. We found a house that we'd like to buy.

Flora: Well, Mr. Baxter, we generally lend 80% of the bank's appraised value on 30-, 35- or 40-year mortgages if the house is less than 10 years old.

Baxter: Oh, it's almost a brand-new house. I think it was built two years ago.

Al: Yes, it's a real good deal. The price is just right.

Flora: Bank appraisals are usually slightly lower than the actual market prices, Mr. Baxter, so you'll have to figure on at least at a 25%—28% down payment.

Al: Yes, we planned on that. We've accumulated enough in our savings for a 30% down payment.

Baxter: What's the interest rate on mortgage loans?

Flora: It fluctuates a little depending on the various factors in the loan, but around 8.75% for longtime clients.

Al: Well, we've been banking here since we got married 8 years ago, Mr. Flora, so I guess we qualify.

Flora: Yes, you certainly do, Mr. Baxter. Let's fill out this application, so we can get started on the paperwork. It takes some time to complete a mortgage loan transaction.

Baxter: We will need title insurance and fire insurance, too, won't we?

Flora: Yes, you will. Here's our mortgage loan booklet which explains all the things which will be necessary.

◎ Useful Expressions

◎ When talking about savings account you may hear:

Do you intend to open a savings account?

I'd like to open a savings account.

I'd like to have a time savings account.

What's the procedure for opening a savings account?

How does one open a savings account?

What's the interest rate for the savings account?

I deposit some money in my savings account.

My savings account draws 5 per cent interest.

I don't collect the interest but plough it back into my savings account.

◎ *When talking about housing loans you may hear:*

We'll need to secure a bank loan.

We are financing for the housing project.

What kinds of materials are needed for a housing loan application?

The bank loan is due this month.

He has applied to the banker for a loan.

He will have to mortgage his land for a loan.

I propose to repay the loan at $20 a month.

The current rate on a 20-year housing loan is 10.25%.

Any natural person having a complete civil capacity may apply for personal commercial housing loan to the bank.

The prospective borrower of personal housing loan should be a natural person having a complete civil capacity.

Housing loans are divided into housing loans on own account, housing loans on authorization and combined loans.

III. The International Monetary Situation

Mary Johnson, an officer of the First National Bank, is discussing the International Monetary System with one of her clients, Harold Black.

Black: I have been reading a great deal recently about exchange-rate fluctuations, payment balances, clean and dirty floats, and the International Monetary System. While I generally understand the way foreign exchange markets work, I am not sure exactly what the International Monetary System is.

Johnson: Well, Mr. Black, the term International Monetary System actually refers to a series of agreements among the major governments and their central banks to bring order and stability to the international exchange markets. The most important, signed in 1944, is called the Bretton Woods Agreement. It established the World Bank and the International Monetary Fund.

Black: Oh, so you mean these agreements regulate international exchange rates?

Johnson: They did until 1971. Up until that time international foreign exchange rates were pegged to fixed values for gold and the U.S dollar, which was considered to be the key currency.

Black: What happened in 1971 to change this?

Johnson: The surplus of dollars abroad from foreign aid, capital exports and chronic balance of payments deficits forced the U.S. to formally suspend gold convertibility. This brought an end to the old Bretton Woods System.

Black: Is that when the Smithsonian Agreement was signed?

Johnson: Yes, in December 1971. Under that and subsequent agreements, the fixed rate exchange system has been changed to a floating exchange rate system in which the value of various currencies fluctuate to restore balance-of-payments equilibrium.

Black: So you mean that foreign exchange rates are now free to change according to the laws of supply and demand?

Johnson: Not quite. Actually, we now have a managed floating exchange rate system, or what many people call a dirty float system. This means that, while there is a great degree of flexibility in exchange rates according to balance of payment factors, central banks still intervene in the market by buying or selling large amounts of foreign currencies to prevent wide-ranging fluctuations.

Black: Why do they do this? Wouldn't a clean float be better?

Johnson: Well, a clean float means that the parity rate of various currencies would go up or go down to restore balance-of-payments equilibrium. Therefore, a country's international trade position could be affected by an appreciation of its currency.

Black: Oh, I see. So governments must consider their internal fiscal and political requirements, too.

Johnson: Yes, that's right. That's why it takes a great deal of international cooperation to make the present system work.

◎ Useful Expressions

◎ When talking about the exchange rate you may hear:

What's your exchange rate for RMB notes today?

Would you please tell me the exchange rate today?

I'll check the exchange rate for U.S. dollars.

The exchange rate is subject to fluctuations.

It comes to 50 U.S. dollars at today's exchange rate.

The exchange rate today is 200 yen to the pound.

Unit 5 Finance

IV. Practicing

1. Match the words and phrases in the left column with the meaning in the right column.

   (1) issue   a. an important subject that people are arguing about or discussing
   b. publish or put into circulation

   (2) currency   a. monetary system in use in a country
   b. state of being in common

   (3) supervise a. excellent
   b. watch or keep a check on something being done to make sure it is done properly

   (4) note   a. short written record to aid memory
   b. piece of paper money issued by a bank

2. Order the following dialogue according to a logical process.

   A: Wait a moment, please.
      OK. Here's your passbook. Thank you.
   B: I'd like to open an account.
   C: OK. Please fill out this form.
      How much do you want to deposit?
   D: One hundred and fifty dollars. Here you are.
   E: What can I do for you?
   F: Thank you.

V. Optional Reading

Banking Operations

John Anderson's girl-friend, Betty Rogers, is a teller at the First National Bank. She is explaining the operation and organization of the bank to John.

Rogers: Our bank is organized into a number of departments, each of which is responsible for a particular area of business. For example, the Trust Department handles investments, the Collateral Department keeps loan records and pledged securities, and the Real Estate Department handles mortgage loans on real estate.

Anderson: What department are you in? You're a teller, aren't you?

Rogers: Yes, I am a paying and receiving teller. We are usually the people who have the

	most contact with our customers. We are part of the Operations Department, the department which takes care of most of the day-to-day business of the bank.
Anderson:	What's the Auditing Department? Isn't that where your friend Alice works?
Rogers:	Yes, Alice is an assistant auditor. The Auditing Department has the responsibility of checking and supervising all of the bank's activities to be sure there are no errors or improper procedures.
Anderson:	Does the Auditing Department keep the main records of all transactions?
Rogers:	No, that's the job of the General Ledger Department. That's the department that is the central bookkeeper for the bank. Of course, modern banks keep such records in computers instead of in ledgers.
Anderson:	Who is the highest officer of the bank?
Rogers:	That's Mr. Sunderland, our president. He is responsible to the Board of Directors, which is elected by the stockholders. He is assisted by the senior vice-presidents, vice-presidents and assistant vice-presidents.
Anderson:	How many vice-presidents do you have?
Rogers:	There are quite a few. Usually each department is headed by a vice-president or an assistant cashier. That's the lowest-ranking officer position in most banks.
Anderson:	Aren't all department managers officers?
Rogers:	No, not all of them are. Actually, the word officer means a person authorized by the board of directors to represent the bank in certain dealings. It doesn't necessarily represent his function in a department. For example, my boss is not a bank officer, he is a chief teller. If we were an officer, his title would be assistant-cashier and chief-teller.
Anderson:	That sounds very confusing. Why don't banks just make all department managers officers?
Rogers:	It's part of the bank's system of assigning authority and responsibility. After all, banks have special obligations to their depositors because we are handling their money, not only our own.
Anderson:	That's right. And I am a depositor, too. I've got $37.50 in my account.

[Company Name]
[Your Company Slogan]

PURCHASE ORDER

[Street Address]
[City, ST ZIP Code]
Phone [(212)444-0123]   Fax [(212)444-0144]

The following number must appear on all related correspondence, shipping papers, and invoices:
P.O. NUMBER: [001] (The number assigned to the purchase order)

Unit 5   Finance

VENDOR: (Supplier Name and Address)
[Name]
[Company]
[Street Address]
[City, ST ZIP Code]
[Phone]

SHIP TO: (Receiving Department address f the buyer)
[Name]
[Company]
[Street Address]
[City, ST ZIP Code]
[Phone]

P.O. DATE	REQUISITIONER	SHIPPED VIA	F.O.B. POINT	TERMS
The date the purchase order was originated	The person who requested the order	Shipping instructions entered by Purchasing Department	Shipping terms defined by Purchasing Department	Payment terms defined by Purchasing Department

QTY	UNIT	DESCRIPTION	UNIT PRICE	TOTAL
Quantity of the good or service	The unit of measurement (e.g.,each,box, lot)	Briefly describes the goods or services being required, all relevant information must be provided to ensure appropriate terms and conditions are applied on the Purchase Order.	Requires the price for each unit of measure.	
			SUBTOTAL	
			SALES TAX	
			SHIPPING & HANDLING	
			OTHER	
			TOTAL	The total amount of all items on the purchase order

Please send two copies of your invoice.

Enter this order in accordance with the prices, terms, delivery method, and specifications listed above.

Please notify us immediately if you are unable to ship as specified.

Send all correspondence to:
  [Name]
  [Street Address]
  [City, ST ZIP Code]
  Phone [(212)444-0123]   Fax [(212)444-0144]

_____
Authorized by   Date

Unit 6　Business Plan

Unit Aims

- To make clear of the conception of the business plan
- To learn more information related to the business plan
- To grasp the structure and understand the text
- To learn the terms used in business planning

Warming Up

- What is a business plan in your opinion?
- What is the function of a business plan in business?

I. Business Plan Writing

Read the following dialogue between Sean and Jack on how to write a business plan.

Sean: Hey, Jack. Is everything going well?

Jack: Oh, I have a big task to do. Sean, do you know how to write a business plan?

Sean: What type of plan are you writing?

Jack: The general manager of our company has asked me to write a business plan about our new investment project.

Sean: Well, the main things you should include are an outline of your idea, your market research and your budgets.

Jack: Oh, I didn't realize that it would be so much work. Is there a quick way instead?

Sean: If you ask someone to invest in your business, they would like to get as much information as possible to ensure their profit.

Jack: OK. I think I really have a lot work to do on it. Would you like to help if I am in trouble with the writing?

Sean: Sure! No problem!

Jack: Oh, you are so kind and helpful. Thanks.

II. What Is a Business Plan

A business plan is a written document describing the nature of the business, the sales and marketing strategy, and the financial background, and containing a projected profit and loss statement.

Different Purposes for Writing Business Plans
- To find out if your business idea is good.
- To serve as a blueprint for developing your business.
- To get a business loan or grant from a traditional institution or lender.
- To attract investors or partners.
- To serve as the basis for business planning and to manage your business's growth.

Outline of a business plan

1. Front cover
2. Statement of purpose
3. Summary
4. Table of contents
5. The business

    Business objectives

    Name, address, contact details and ABN

    Business activity, commencement date, commencement capital and business structure

    Competitive advantage

    Owners' profiles

    Major clients

    Licences and registrations

    Business advisors

    Current performance

6. Industry analysis

    ANZSIC category, political/economic, social, technological, industry and competition

    Key success factors

7. Product and services

    Product range analysis

    Competitor analysis

    SWOT analysis

8. Marketing plan

    Target market

    Marketing objectives

Marketing strategy—product, price, promotion and place
9. Operational strategy
   Location and premises
   Plant and equipment
   Inventory
   Human resources
   Environmental strategy
10. Financial strategy
    Financial objectives
    Capital structure
    Statements of financial performance and financial position
    Cashflow forecasts
    Sales and collections from debtors forecasts
    Purchases and payments to creditors forecasts
    Breakeven analysis
11. Appendices
    Financial statements
    Legal documents, leases, contacts, letters of intent
    Research documents, patents, trademarks

(From www.smallbusiness.wa.gov.au)

III. Reading

It's a truism that every business needs a business plan. But that business plan's form and content should depend on the business plan's purpose. Ask yourself why you need a business plan and what your need is before you write one, and tailor your business plan to your purpose. A good plan is one that suits your business and provides efficiency.

The business plan is the blueprint for your business. You wouldn't walk over to an empty lot and just start nailing boards together if you wanted to build a house. Starting a business without a business plan is just as foolish.

Yet unlike a house, a business isn't static. We often make the mistake of thinking of a business plan as a single, static document that you just put together when you're first starting out and then set aside.

In actuality, the business plan for any business will change over time as the business develops, and any particular business may have multiple business plans as its objectives change.

Here are five good reasons why you should write a business plan.

1) To test the feasibility of your business idea.

Writing a business plan is the best way to test whether or not an idea for starting a business is feasible, other than going out and doing it. In this sense, the business plan is your safety net; writing a business plan can save you a great deal of time and money if working through the business plan reveals that your business idea is untenable. Often, an idea for starting a business is discarded at the marketing analysis or competitive analysis stage, freeing you to move on to a new (and better) idea.

2) To give your new business the best possible chance of success.

Writing a business plan will ensure that you pay attention to both the broad operational and financial objectives of your new business and the details, such as budgeting and market planning. Taking the time to work through the process of writing a business plan will make for a smoother startup period and fewer unforeseen problems as your business becomes established.

3) To secure funding, such as bank loans.

You're going to need both operating and startup capital to start a new business and you have no hope of getting any money from established financial institutions such as banks without a well developed business plan. And established businesses often need money, too, to do things such as buy new equipment or property, or because of market downturns. Having a business plan gives you a much better chance of getting the money you need to keep operating or to expand.

4) To make business planning manageable and effective.

A business plan is essential if you're thinking of starting a business, but it's also an important tool for established businesses. Viable businesses are dynamic; they change and grow. The company's original business plan needs to be revised as new goals are set. Reviewing the business plan can also help you see what goals have been accomplished, what changes need to be made, or what new directions your company's growth should take.

5) To attract investors.

Whether you want to shop your business to venture capitalists, or attract angel investors, you need to have a solid business plan. A presentation may pique their interest, but they'll need a well-written document they can take away and study before they'll be prepared to make any investment commitment.

Be prepared for your business plan to be scrutinized; both venture capitalists and angel investors will want to conduct extensive background checks and competitive analysis to be certain that what's written in your business plan is indeed the case.

Writing a business plan is time-consuming, but it's essential if you want to have a successful business that's going to survive the startup phase. If your business doesn't have one, maybe it's time to start working on one. The process of writing a business plan can do wonders to clarify where you've been and where you're going.

A business plan is considered to be the most effective tool used by entrepreneurs to attract business investors to fund their business. How much capital a company can raise often depends on the effectiveness of the business plan. A business plan in other words has to be a well-structured document that will help you in securing funds from venture capitalists, banks and other investors and lending agencies to help finance your business.

There are some essentials that need to be followed while writing down a business plan to attract a business investor or a venture capitalist. Some of these include:

A convincing introduction: In order to attract venture capital funding, it is essential to include an introduction or an executive summary that is convincing and has the potential to create an impact on the investor, so that he gets motivated to invest into the venture.

A well structured body: Although the executive summary is something that attracts investors the most, the body of the plan needs to convey the meaning and the purpose of the business. The different sections such as nature of the business, market and competitor analysis, management team and the company's marketing strategy is what attracts more venture capital funding.

The USP of the business: In order to attract investors, a very important thing the entrepreneur should do is highlight the unique aspect of the business, popularly called the unique selling proposition. For example, an Internet-based business should focus on how much of traffic it is generating. Some companies highlight on how its products/services is different from its competitors, some focus on the marketing strategies, corporate social responsibilities and so on. Whatever the USP is, the plan should be able to persuade the potential venture capitalist that it has the potential to make profit and make some difference in the market with the help of its products/services.

An interesting layout: Many entrepreneurs tend to ignore this aspect of a business plan, but it often creates an impact to venture capitalists. A typical business plan has a boring layout. However, successful plans often have interesting layouts with short paragraphs, use of appropriate bullets and judicious use of colors, images and pie charts, alongside relevant information.

A good packaging: A good packaging of the business plan is essential to attract venture capital funding. There are three types of summaries that attract investors, and these needs to be highlighted. These include: executive summary, management summary and financial summary. Once these are packaged well and presented before the investors, you can be assured of raising capitals for your business. A cover letter requesting for funds is also very important and has to be written in meticulously.

Investors look for realistic plans. So, one should not come up with a highly optimistic financial projection as such plans may get rejected outright.

Unit 6　Business Plan

◎ **Useful Words**

static	[ˈstætɪk]	adj.	静止的,不变的
multiple	[ˈmʌltɪp(ə)l]	adj.	多个的,由多个组成的,多重的
feasibility	[ˌfizəˈbɪləti]	n.	可行性,可能性
untenable	[ʌnˈtenəb(ə)l]	adj.	(论据等)站不住脚的,不能维持的
discard	[dɪˈskɑːd]	v.	抛弃,放弃,丢弃
operational	[ɒpəˈreɪʃ(ə)n(ə)l]	adj.	操作的,运作的
unforeseen	[ʌnfɔːˈsiːn]	adj.	未预见到的,无法预料的
downturn	[ˈdaʊntɜːn]	n.	衰退(经济方面),低迷时期
manageable	[ˈmænɪdʒəb(ə)l]	adj.	易管理的,易控制的,易办的
viable	[ˈvaɪəbl]	adj.	实际可行的,能成功的,可获胜的
dynamic	[daɪˈnæmɪk]	adj.	动态的,动力的,有活力的
revise	[rɪˈvaɪz]	v.	修订,校订
solid	[ˈsɒlɪd]	adj.	固体的,可靠的
pique	[piːk]	v.	刺激,伤害……自尊心,激怒
scrutinize	[ˈskruːtənaɪz]	v.	细看,细读,详察,仔细观察(或检察)
clarify	[ˈklærɪfaɪ]	v.	澄清,说明,阐明,讲清楚
entrepreneur	[ˌɒntrəprəˈnɜː]	n.	企业家,承包人,主办者
fund	[fʌnd]	v.	投资,资助
convincing	[kənˈvɪnsɪŋ]	adj.	令人信服的,有说服力的
highlight	[ˈhaɪlaɪt]	v.	突出,强调,使显著,加亮
traffic	[ˈtræfɪk]	v.	交易,贸易
layout	[ˈleɪaʊt]	n.	布局,设计,安排,陈列
judicious	[dʒuːˈdɪʃəs]	adj.	明智的,头脑精明的,判断正确的
alongside	[əlɒŋˈsaɪd]	adv.	在旁边
meticulously	[meˈtɪkjuləsli]	adv.	细致地,一丝不苟地,拘泥地
projection	[prəˈdʒekʃ(ə)n]	n.	规划,预测

IV. Practicing

1. Here are ten terms contained in a business plan, match each of the term with the right statement of the meaning, and write down the letter in the bracket.

   (1) Business Plan (　　)
   (2) Executive Summary (　　)
   (3) Market Analysis (　　)
   (4) Company Description (　　)

(5) Organization and Management (   )

(6) Marketing and Sales Management (   )

(7) Service or Product Line (   )

(8) Funding Request (   )

(9) Financial Analysis (   )

(10) Appendix (   )

a. Nature of business. Primary factors that you believe will make your company successful. Marketplace needs that you are trying to satisfy, how your product will meet those needs and potential customers.

b. Define your marketing strategy, penetration, growth strategy, channels of distribution, communication strategy, the overall sales strategy.

c. The mission statement. Description of the business. Summary of the managements future plans. Summary of company growth.

d. A roadmap leads to success. Help with the achievements of your goals.

e. Industry description and analysis. Identify the target market.

f. NOT REQUIRED! Display important documents eg. resumes, letters of reference, and legal documents.

f. What you sell, what's unique about it, what's your solution for the target market which you want to satisfy. Data about suppliers, and product availability. "Secret Info" Patents.

h. Company's organizational structure, details about the ownership of your company, profiles of your management team, and the qualifications of your board of directors.

i. Financials developed after one has analyzed the market and set clear objectives.

j. Current needs, future needs, potential changes/ impacts to income stream.

2. **Fill in the blanks with words and phrases given in the word bank. Change the form where necessary.**

viable	untenable	unforeseen	set aside	downturn
revised	clarify solid	pique	entrepreneur	convincing
funded	highlighted	layout	judicious	

(1) Governments need a credible plan to _____ enough resources in the future to repay the additional public debt their stimulus has added.

(2) We are at the start of what the experts say may be the most severe global financial crisis and economic _____ seen since the Great Depression began in 1929.

(3) I find your theory is _____ and it must be rejected.

(4) Plans sometimes do not work out, people don't behave as expected and _____ obstacles

might stand in the way.

(5) Nevertheless, an equitable commitment can and should exist for every phase of the project if the project is to remain _____.

(6) The English textbooks for middle schools have been completely _____.

(7) My theory is established on the _____ basis of facts.

(8) Another way to _____ your child's interest is to give him a book that inspired a movie.

(9) I hope that what I say will _____ the situation.

(10) Last year Collins wrote a moving ballad which _____ the plight of the homeless.

(11) If you're an _____ or small business owner, you might not make any real money until you sell your business.

(12) The airport is being privately _____ by a construction group.

(13) Scientists say there is no _____ evidence that power lines have anything to do with cancer.

(14) This map shows the _____ of the plant.

(15) Laura is very _____ as she saves her money in the bank.

3. Choose the best word to fill in the blank in each sentence with the help of the equivalent meaning of the word given in the bracket, and understand the meaning of the sentences about business plan.

(1) A good business plan defines your business and _____ (= describes/lists) your goals.
   A. identifies   B. idents   C. idealizes

(2) A lot _____ (= depends) upon how comprehensive your business plan is.
   A. hinges   B. haggles   C. hassles

(3) A list of your assets, liabilities and net worth is what's known as a _____ sheet.
   A. balanced   B. balancing   C. balance

(4) Many new business owners rely on _____ (= funding from other sources, not their own) to start and develop their business.
   A. outer funding   B. outside funding C. other funds

(5) How do you plan to get the financial _____ (= money, etc.) to start your business?
   A. recourse   B. recurrence   C. resources

(6) A cash _____ analysis is an analysis of a company's financial "health."
   A. flow   B. flowing   C. flood

(7) You shouldn't _____ when it comes to drawing up a business plan. (= You shouldn't take too long to finish it.)
   A. drag your feet   B. drag your shoes C. drag it along

(8) We have a well _____ vision for our business.
   A. thought   B. strong   C. thought-out

(9) Your business' _____ refers to how easy (or difficult) it is to market/promote it.

    A. market savvy   B. marketability   C. market watch

(10) Any bank will want to make sure your business has a good chance of being _____ before giving you a loan.

    A. profit-oriented   B. profitable   C. profit-sharing

(From businessenglishsite.com)

V. Optional Reading

Business Plan Essentials

When you're about to embark on developing a business plan, remember this: Form follows function, so you want a plan that fits your exact business needs. The emphasis should change depending on whether it's a plan for starting a company, raising investment money, supporting a business loan or managing an existing business.

In most cases, your plan will be a 20-to-30-page document written in simple business language so it's easy to read with the main points highlighted and lots of bullets, and some tables and charts to highlight the most important financial projections. A standard plan includes seven sections:

1. The Executive Summary. Write this summary last, and make sure it contains the highlights of your plan. Assume your most important readers will read only this section.

2. The Company. A plan for a startup describes your strategy for creating the legal entity and how the initial ownership will be divided among the founders. It should also include a table that lists startup costs and initial funding. A plan for an ongoing or already existing company should describe the legal form of the business, the company history and the business's past performance.

3. What You Sell. Describe the products or services you offer. Emphasize why buyers purchase those things, what benefits they get, and what pain points they have before they buy. Show how much it costs to deliver what you're selling.

4. Your Market. Describe your target market, including market demographics, market growth and trends. Include a table that shows a market forecast. Describe the nature of your industry and the competition you have.

5. Strategy and Implementation. Strategy is all about focus. So focus on certain target market segments, certain products or services, and specific distribution avenues. Forecast your sales and the cost of sales. Define your milestones with dates, budgets and specific responsibilities.

6. Management Team. Name and describe the key members on your team. Include a table

that shows personnel costs. List the gaps in the management team—if any—and show how they're being addressed.

7. Financial Projections. Describe your financial strategy and how it supports your projected growth. Include a break-even analysis that shows risk as a matter of fixed vs. variable costs. Include projected profit or loss, cash flow and balance sheets.

As you deal with these standard sections, remember that this is your plan and not a classroom assignment, which means you should ignore anything that doesn't fit your needs. For example, if you're developing a business plan for internal use only that won't be read by anybody outside the company, you don't need to describe your company history. You might want to include management team gaps and a personnel plan, but you probably don't need to describe the background of your key management team members.

Making your plan fit your needs means you might add some things, too, beyond the standard outline. For example, a plan for investors should include the investment offering—how much equity for how much money—as well as a discussion of exit strategy, use of funds and return on investment. A plan supporting a bank loan application needs to describe the loan requirements, intended use of funds, collateral and repayment plans.

So what should every plan include no matter what? There are three essentials:

1. Specific milestones, with deadline dates, spending budgets and a list of the people responsible for them. I've seen this called "weaving a MAT," with MAT standing for "milestones, assumptions and tasks." That normally goes into Section 5, Strategy and Implementation. Make the responsibilities specific for specific people, and make sure every task gets assigned to a single person with a name and a face. This section must describe how these different milestones are going to be tracked and measured.

2. Real cash flow. Your plan should show cash flow—either projected or actual or both—month by month for at least 12 months. Show where you're getting money and how much, and show what you're spending the money on. This is cash flow, not just profit and loss, and you have to understand how different cash flow is from profits. Profitable companies go under all the time, but companies with positive cash flow can pay their bills.

3. Focus. A business plan should establish your company's priorities. Don't try to do everything, and don't try to please everybody.

The author is an Entrepreneur contributor. The opinions expressed are those of the writer.
(Read more: http://www.entrepreneur.com/article/76482#ixzz2tGaCFg17)

Unit 7　The Financial Statement

Unit Aims

- To know the structure of the financial statement
- To know the content of the financial statement
- To know how to make a financial statement
- To master the basic expressions of the financial statement

Warming Up

- Find out the structure of the financial statement.
- Use all the resources you can find and discuss with your classmates to know how to make a financial statement.

I. The Balance Sheet

1. Dialogue

Read the following dialogue and try to understand what is the financial statement and what are the basic financial statements.

(S: the secretary; A: the accounting)

S:　Excuse me, Miss Green. Mr. Smith wants you to show him the financial statement of our company.

A:　Oh, my God. I haven't finished it yet. Did he say when it is due?

S:　Don't worry. Mr. Smith said that you could hand it in tomorrow.

A: Thank God!

S: By the way, Miss Green, what is the financial statement?

A: Oh, in short, that is a summary report that shows how a firm has used the funds entrusted to it by its stockholders and lenders, and what is its current financial position.

S: I see it. It is just one small report. I am sure you can finish it in a minute.

A: No, no. There are three basic financial statements. The first one is the balance sheet, which shows the firm's assets, liabilities, and net worth on a stated date.

S: And the second?

A: The second one is the income statement, which shows how the net income of the firm is arrived at over a stated period.

S: I guess the last one is concerned with the cash.

A: Yes, you are right. It is called the cash flow statement, which shows the inflows and outflows of cash caused by the firm's activities during a stated period. They are also called business financials.

S: I assume you should do a lot with the numbers. I won't waste your time. Good luck!

◎ *Useful Expressions*

financial statement	财务报表
balance sheet	资产负债表
income statement	利润表(损益表)
cash flow statement	现金流量表

2. The Balance Sheet

In financial accounting, a balance sheet or statement of financial position is a statement of the financial position of a business which states the assets, liabilities, and the owners' equity at a particular date, such as the end of its financial year. The date is often referred as balance sheet date. Of the three basic financial statements, the balance sheet is the only statement which applies to a single point in time of a business' calendar year.

To make students understand the balance sheet more easily, we provide the Red Hat's balance sheet as follows:

RED HAT, INC.
CONSOLIDATED BALANCE SHEETS
(In thousands—except share and per share amounts)

	August 31, 2013 (Unaudited)	February 28, 2013 (1)
Current assets:		
Cash and cash equivalents	$ 596,794	$ 487,084
Investments in debt and equity securities, short-term	266,841	392,381
Accounts receivable, net of allowances for doubtful accounts of $1,540 and $1,339, respectively	232,884	302,942
Deferred tax assets, net	88,325	88,765
Prepaid expenses	93,987	94,421
Other current assets	2,829	3,156
Total current assets	$ 1,281,660	$ 1,368,749
Property and equipment, net of accumulated depreciation and amortization of $206,734 and $189,985, respectively	167,343	141,586
Goodwill	690,342	690,911
Identifiable intangibles, net	142,247	142,243
Investments in debt securities, long-term	427,036	438,908
Other assets, net	30,953	31,263
Total assets	$ 2,739,581	$ 2,813,660
LIABILITIES AND STOCKHOLDERS' EQUITY		
Current liabilities:		
Accounts payable and accrued expenses	$ 178,904	$ 154,202
Deferred revenue	796,044	830,486
Other current obligations	993	1,024
Total current liabilities	$ 975,941	$ 985,712
Long-term deferred revenue	263,553	259,466
Other long-term obligations	58,483	48,321
Commitments and contingencies (NOTES 12 and 13)		
Stockholders' equity:		
Preferred stock, 5,000,000 shares authorized, none outstanding	—	—

Common stock, $0.0001 per share par value, 300,000,000 shares authorized, 229,781,265 and 229,210,961 shares issued, and 189,498,113 and 193,021,226 shares outstanding at August 31, 2013 and February 28, 2013, respectively	23	23
Additional paid-in capital	1,846,825	1,802,899
Retained earnings	623,079	541,880
Treasury stock at cost, 40,283,152 and 36,189,735 shares at August 31, 2013 and February 28, 2013, respectively	(1,016,401)	(816,674)
Accumulated other comprehensive loss	(11,922)	(7,967)
Total stockholders' equity	$ 1,441,604	$ 1,520,161
Total liabilities and stockholders' equity	$ 2,739,581	$ 2,813,660

(1) Derived from audited financial statements.

The accompanying notes are an integral part of these consolidated financial statements.

(数据来源：http://www.sec.gov/Archives/edgar/data/1087423/000119312513391600/d574178d10q.htm)

II. The Income Sheet

The income sheet reports the results of a company's operations for a period of time (a month, a quarter, or a year). It summarizes the revenues and the costs (expenses) to produce the "results" of an income statement: net income or net loss. The income statement shows three accounting elements: revenue, expense, and the profit. People consider the income sheet important because it can answer the question of profitability of a business.

RED HAT, INC.
CONSOLIDATED STATEMENTS OF COMPREHENSIVE INCOME
(In thousands)
(Unaudited)

	Three Months Ended		Six Months Ended	
	August 31, 2013	August 31, 2012	August 31, 2013	August 31, 2012
Net income	$ 40,808	$ 35,005	$ 81,199	$ 72,466
Other comprehensive income (loss):				

Change in foreign currency translation adjustment	1,567	1,242	(2,049)	(8,078)
Available-for-sale securities (net of tax):				
Unrealized gain (loss) on available-for-sale securities during the period	(1,230)	1,252	(1,589)	1,297
Reclassification for gain realized on available-for-sale securities, reported in other income (expense), net	(31)	(15)	(317)	(379)
Net change in available-for-sale securities (net of tax)	(1,261)	1,237	(1,906)	918
Total other comprehensive income (loss)	306	2,479	(3,955)	(7,160)
Comprehensive income	$ 41,114	$ 37,484	$ 77,244	$ 65,306

The accompanying notes are an integral part of these consolidated financial statements.

(数据来源：http://www.sec.gov/Archives/edgar/data/1087423/000119312513391600/d574178d10q.htm)

III. The Cash Flow Statement

The cash flow statement provides information about the cash receipts (inflows) and cash payments (outflows) during a period. The cash flow statement shows three categories of cash flows: the cash flows from the operating activities; the cash flows from the investing activities; the cash flows from the financing activities.

Information in the cash flow statement helps answer questions such as:

1) How does a company obtain its cash?
2) Where does a company spend its cash?
3) What is the changes in the cash balance?

Unit 7 The Financial Statement

RED HAT, INC.
CONSOLIDATED STATEMENTS OF CASH FLOWS
(In thousands)
(Unaudited)

	Three Months Ended		Six Months Ended	
	August 31, 2013	August 31, 2012	August 31, 2013	August 31, 2012
Cash flows from operating activities:				
Net income	$ 40,808	$ 35,005	$ 81,199	$ 72,466
Adjustments to reconcile net income to net cash provided by operating activities:				
Depreciation and amortization	18,439	14,568	36,371	28,647
Share-based compensation expense	29,874	23,859	53,006	46,065
Deferred income taxes	3,818	13,036	16,663	23,063
Excess tax benefits from share-based payment arrangements	(2,610)	(9,600)	(5,643)	(19,800)
Net amortization of bond premium on debt securities available for sale	2,285	1,748	4,336	3,420
Other	(96)	529	47	(1,840)
Changes in operating assets and liabilities net of effects of acquisitions:				
Accounts receivable	(6,341)	(18,735)	66,081	35,825
Prepaid expenses	(5,645)	833	(2,394)	(6,966)
Accounts payable and accrued expenses	38,902	13,502	26,293	22,928
Deferred revenue	1,880	26,430	(15,020)	21,308
Other	(2,385)	2,678	(195)	3,141
Net cash provided by operating activities	118,929	103,853	260,744	228,257
Cash flows from investing activities:				
Purchase of investment in debt securities available for sale	(217,433)	(185,028)	(347,076)	(507,769)
Proceeds from sales and maturities of investment in debt securities available for sale	153,917	190,094	479,767	417,779
Acquisition of business, net of cash acquired	—	(10,051)	—	(10,051)
Purchase of other intangible assets	(10,177)	(24,341)	(12,521)	(26,863)
Purchase of property and equipment	(21,829)	(20,344)	(48,506)	(36,243)
Other	(2,126)	—	(1,934)	330

Net cash provided by (used in) investing activities	(97,648)	(49,670)	69,730	(162,817)
Cash flows from financing activities:				
Excess tax benefits from share-based payment arrangements	2,610	9,600	5,643	19,800
Proceeds from exercise of common stock options	635	2,626	1,088	6,516
Payments related to net settlement of share-based compensation awards	(3,833)	(3,856)	(14,815)	(22,688)
Purchase of treasury stock	(20,009)	(2,871)	(199,345)	(32,882)
Payments on other borrowings	(312)	(213)	(617)	(477)
Net cash provided by (used in) financing activities	(20,909)	5,286	(208,046)	(29,731)
Effect of foreign currency exchange rates on cash and cash equivalents	(1,576)	3,491	(12,718)	(13,350)
Net increase (decrease) in cash and cash equivalents	(1,204)	62,960	109,710	22,359
Cash and cash equivalents at beginning of the period	597,998	508,616	487,084	549,217
Cash and cash equivalents at end of the period	$ 596,794	$ 571,576	$ 596,794	$ 571,576

The accompanying notes are an integral part of these consolidated financial statements.

(数据来源：http://www.sec.gov/Archives/edgar/data/1087423/000119312513391600/d574178d10q.htm)

IV. Practicing

1. Fill in the blanks with the exact words you have read in Part I, and II.

(1) A standard company balance sheet has three parts: _____, _____ and _____.

(2) The way to look at the balance sheet equation is that _____.

(3) A business operating entirely in cash can measure its profits by_____.

(4) An income statement can show the company's _____ during a particular period.

(5) An income statement indicates how the _____ are transformed into _____.

(6) What are the two methods that we can use to prepare an income statement?

2. Answer the following questions.

(1) What are the functions of a cash flow statement?

(2) What kind of people or groups are interested in cash flow statements?

Unit 7 The Financial Statement

V. Optional Reading

IAS 1 (2007) Presentation of Financial Statements
Key Notes for SOCI and SOFS

Statement of Financial Position (Balance Sheet)

An entity must normally present a classified statement of financial position, separating current and non-current assets and liabilities. Only if a presentation based on liquidity provides information that is reliable and more relevant may the current/non-current split be omitted. [IAS 1.60] In either case, if an asset (liability) category combines amounts that will be received (settled) after 12 months with assets (liabilities) that will be received (settled) within 12 months, note disclosure is required that separates the longer-term amounts from the 12-month amounts. [IAS 1.61]

Current assets are cash; cash equivalent; assets held for collection, sale, or consumption within the entity's normal operating cycle; or assets held for trading within the next 12 months. All other assets are non-current. [IAS 1.66]

Current liabilities are those to be settled within the entity's normal operating cycle or due within 12 months, or those held for trading, or those for which the entity does not have an unconditional right to defer payment beyond 12 months. Other liabilities are non-current. [IAS 1.69]

When a long-term debt is expected to be refinanced under an existing loan facility and the entity has the discretion the debt is classified as non-current, even if due within 12 months. [IAS 1.73]

If a liability has become payable on demand because an entity has breached an undertaking under a long-term loan agreement on or before the reporting date, the liability is current, even if the lender has agreed, after the reporting date and before the authorization of the financial statements for issue, not to demand payment as a consequence of the breach. [IAS 1.74] However, the liability is classified as non-current if the lender agreed by the reporting date to provide a period of grace ending at least 12 months after the end of the reporting period, within which the entity can rectify the breach and during which the lender cannot demand immediate repayment. [IAS 1.75]

Minimum items on the face of the statement of financial position [IAS 1.54]
- (a) property, plant and equipment
- (b) investment property
- (c) intangible assets
- (d) financial assets (excluding amounts shown under (e), (h), and (i))

- (e) investments accounted for using the equity method
- (f) biological assets
- (g) inventories
- (h) trade and other receivables
- (i) cash and cash equivalents
- (j) assets held for sale
- (k) trade and other payables
- (l) provisions
- (m) financial liabilities (excluding amounts shown under (k) and (l))
- (n) liabilities and assets for current tax, as defined in IAS 12
- (o) deferred tax liabilities and deferred tax assets, as defined in IAS 12
- (p) liabilities included in disposal groups
- (q) non-controlling interests , presented within equity and
- (r) issued capital and reserves attributable to owners of the parent

Additional line items may be needed to fairly present the entity's financial position. [IAS 1.54]

IAS 1 does not prescribe the format of the balance sheet. Assets can be presented current then non-current, or vice versa, and liabilities and equity can be presented current then non-current then equity, or vice versa. A net asset presentation (assets minus liabilities) is allowed. The long-term financing approach used in UK and elsewhere—fixed assets + current assets —short term payables = long-term debt plus equity—is also acceptable.

Regarding issued share capital and reserves, the following disclosures are required: [IAS 1.79]

- numbers of shares authorized, issued and fully paid, and issued but not fully paid
- par value
- reconciliation of shares outstanding at the beginning and the end of the period
- description of rights, preferences, and restrictions
- treasury shares, including shares held by subsidiaries and associates
- shares reserved for issuance under options and contracts
- a description of the nature and purpose of each reserve within equity

Statement of Comprehensive Income

Comprehensive income for a period includes profit or loss for that period plus other comprehensive income recognized in that period. As a result of the 2003 revision to IAS 1, the Standard is now using "profit or loss" rather than "net profit or loss" as the descriptive term for the bottom line of the income statement.

Unit 7   The Financial Statement

All items of income and expense recognized in a period must be included in profit or loss unless a Standard or an Interpretation requires otherwise. [IAS 1.88] Some IFRSs require or permit that some components to be excluded from profit or loss and instead to be included in other comprehensive income. [IAS 1.89]

The components of other comprehensive income include:
- changes in revaluation surplus (IAS 16 and IAS 38)
- actuarial gains and losses on defined benefit plans recognized in accordance with IAS 19
- gains and losses arising from translating the financial statements of a foreign operation (IAS 21)
- gains and losses on remeasuring available-for-sale financial assets (IAS 39)
- the effective portion of gains and losses on hedging instruments in a cash flow hedge (IAS 39).

An entity has a choice of presenting:
- a single statement of comprehensive income or
- two statements:
    an income statement displaying components of profit or loss and
    a statement of comprehensive income that begins with profit or loss (bottom line of the income statement) and displays components of other comprehensive income [IAS 1.81]

Minimum items on the face of the statement of comprehensive income should include: [IAS 1.82]
- revenue
- finance costs
- share of the profit or loss of associates and joint ventures accounted for using the equity method
- tax expense
- a single amount comprising the total of (i) the post-tax profit or loss of discontinued operations and (ii) the post-tax gain or loss recognised on the disposal of the assets or disposal group(s) constituting the discontinued operation
- profit or loss
- each component of other comprehensive income classified by nature
- share of the other comprehensive income of associates and joint ventures accounted for using the equity method
- total comprehensive income

The following items must also be disclosed in the statement of comprehensive income as allocations for the period: [IAS 1.83]

- profit or loss for the period attributable to non-controlling interests and owners of the parent
- total comprehensive income attributable to non-controlling interests and owners of the parent

Additional line items may be needed to fairly present the entity's results of operations. [IAS 1.85]

No items may be presented in the statement of comprehensive income (or in the income statement, if separately presented) or in the notes as "extraordinary items." [IAS 1.87]

Certain items must be disclosed separately either in the statement of comprehensive income or in the notes, if material, including: [IAS 1.98]

- write-downs of inventories to net realizable value or of property, plant and equipment to recoverable amount, as well as reversals of such write-downs
- restructurings of the activities of an entity and reversals of any provisions for the costs of restructuring
- disposals of items of property, plant and equipment
- disposals of investments
- discontinuing operations
- litigation settlements
- other reversals of provisions

Expenses recognized in profit or loss should be analyzed either by nature (raw materials, staffing costs, depreciation, etc.) or by function (cost of sales, selling, administrative, etc). [IAS 1.99] If an entity categorizes by function, then additional information on the nature of expenses —at a minimum depreciation, amortization and employee benefits expense—must be disclosed. [IAS 1.104]

（文本来源：WWW.IASPLUS.COM）

Note:

IAS: International Accounting Standard《国际会计准则》

Unit 8　E-commerce

Unit Aims

- To understand the conception of e-commerce
- To learn more background information related to e-commerce
- To know the development of e-commerce
- To master the useful vocabulary and terms related to e-commerce

Warming Up

- Do you like shopping? How often do you shop?
- How much do you know about shopping-online?
- How do people purchase online?
- Which do you prefer, shopping in stores or online ? And give your reasons.

I. How to Shop Online

Read the following dialogue and find out how to shop online.

Sue: Jerry, do you know how to shop online? Is it the same with shopping in the store?

Jerry: Not exactly. You need to register to become an affiliate first if you shop online.

Sue: Oh, I got it. And then how to buy things?

Jerry: Once you get in with your affiliate identity, you can buy anything you like.

Sue: Then how to choose the goods I want?

Jerry: Go through the website to search for the goods you want to buy. Take the clothes for example. There are many pictures and details about this product. Choose one you like and input the amount in the text box, and click the "order" button.

Sue: But how to know what goods I have chosen?

Jerry: Some websites offer hyperlink signed add to cart. If you click it, the "cart dialog box" will appear.

Sue: Can I cancel the order of the goods if I don't want to buy?
Jerry: There are many modifying buttons in the "cart dialog box." You can rechoose or cancel before paying. All goods have the same choices.
Sue: That sounds good. Can I have a try?
Jerry: Of course. Once you can operate, you will find it very convenient to purchase.

II. What Is E-commerce?

Electronic commerce, commonly known as e-commerce or eCommerce, consists of the buying and selling of products or services over electronic systems such as the Internet and other computer networks. The amount of trade conducted electronically has grown extraordinarily since the spread of the Internet. A wide variety of commerce is conducted in this way, spurring and drawing on innovations in electronic funds transfer, supply chain management, Internet marketing, online transaction processing, electronic data interchange (EDI), inventory management systems, and automated data collection systems. Modern electronic commerce typically uses the World Wide Web at least at some point in the transaction's lifecycle, although it can encompass a wider range of technologies such as e-mail as well. A large percentage of electronic commerce is conducted entirely electronically for virtual items such as access to premium content on a website, but most electronic commerce involves the transportation of physical items in some way. Online retailers are sometimes known as e-tailers and online retail is sometimes known as e-tail. Almost all big retailers have electronic commerce presence on the World Wide Web. Electronic commerce that is conducted between businesses is referred to as business-to-business or B2B. B2B can be open to all interested parties (e.g. commodity exchange) or limited to specific, pre-qualified participants (private electronic market). Electronic commerce that is conducted between businesses and consumers, on the other hand, is referred to as business-to-consumer or B2C. This is the type of electronic commerce conducted by companies such as Amazon. Electronic commerce is generally considered to be the sales aspect of e-business. It also consists of the exchange of data to facilitate the financing and payment aspects of the business transactions.

◎ **Useful Expressions**

electronic funds transfer	电子资金转账
supply chain management	供应连锁管理
Internet marketing	网络营销
online transaction processing (OLTP)	线上交易处理
electronic data interchange (EDI)	电子数据交换

inventory management	存货管理
automated data collection	自动资料搜集
virtual	虚拟的
premium content	高级内容
e-tailer	电子零售
online retail	在线零售
B2B(Business-to-Business)	企业间的电子商务
B2C(Business-to-Consumer)	企业对消费者的电子商务
C2C (Consumer-to-Consumer)	消费者对消费者的电子商务

III. Reading

The Development of E-commerce

A perfect market
May 13th 2004
From *The Economist* print edition

E-commerce is coming of age, says Paul Markillie, but not in the way predicted in the bubble years.

When the technology bubble burst in 2000, the crazy valuations for online companies vanished with it, and many businesses folded. The survivors plugged on as best they could, encouraged by the growing number of internet users. Now valuations are rising again and some of the dotcoms are making real profits, but the business world has become much more cautious about the internet's potential. The funny thing is that the wild predictions made at the height of the boom—namely, that vast chunks of the world economy would move into cyberspace—are, in one way or another, coming true.

E-commerce is already very big, and it is going to get much bigger. But the actual value of transactions currently concluded online is dwarfed by the extraordinary influence the internet is exerting over purchases carried out in the offline world. That influence is becoming an integral part of e-commerce.

To start with, the internet is profoundly changing consumer behaviour. One in five customers walking into a Sears department store in America to buy an electrical appliance will have researched their purchase online—and most will know down to a dime what they intend to pay. More surprisingly, three out of four Americans start shopping for new cars online, even though most end up buying them from traditional dealers. The difference is that these customers come to the showroom armed with information about the car and the best available deals. Sometimes they even have computer print-outs identifying the particular vehicle from the dealer's stock that they want to buy.

Half of the 60m consumers in Europe who have an internet connection bought products offline after having investigated prices and details online, according to a study by Forrester, a research consultancy. Different countries have different habits. In Italy and Spain, for instance, people are twice as likely to buy offline as online after researching on the internet. But in Britain and Germany, the two most developed internet markets, the numbers are evenly split. Forrester says that people begin to shop online for simple, predictable products, such as DVDs, and then graduate to more complex items. Used-car sales are now one of the biggest online growth areas in America.

Why websites matter?

This has enormous implications for business. A company that neglects its website may be committing commercial suicide. A website is increasingly becoming the gateway to a company's brand, products and services—even if the firm does not sell online. A useless website suggests a useless company, and a rival is only a mouse-click away. But even the coolest website will be lost in cyberspace if people cannot find it, so companies have to ensure that they appear high up in internet search results.

For many users, a search site is now their point of entry to the internet. The best-known search engine has already entered the lexicon: people say they have "Googled" a company, a product or their plumber. The search business has also developed one of the most effective forms of advertising on the internet. And it is already the best way to reach some consumers: teenagers and young men spend more time online than watching television. All this means that search is turning into the internet's next big battleground as Google defends itself against challenges from Yahoo! and Microsoft.

The other way to get noticed online is to offer goods and services through one of the big sites that already get a lot of traffic. Ebay, Yahoo! and Amazon are becoming huge trading platforms for other companies. But to take part, a company's products have to stand up to intense price competition. People check online prices, compare them with those in their local high street and may well take a peek at what customers in other countries are paying. Even if websites are prevented from shipping their goods abroad, there are plenty of web-based entrepreneurs ready to oblige.

What is going on here is arbitrage between different sales channels, says Mohanbir Sawhney, professor of technology at the Kellogg School of Management in Chicago. For instance, someone might use the internet to research digital cameras, but visit a photographic shop for a hands-on demonstration. "I'll think about it," they will tell the sales assistant. Back home, they will use a search engine to find the lowest price and buy online. In this way, consumers are "deconstructing the purchasing process," says Professor Sawhney. They are unbundling product information from the transaction itself.

It is not only price transparency that makes internet consumers so powerful; it is also the way the net makes it easy for them to be fickle. If they do not like a website, they swiftly move on. "The web is the most selfish environment in the world," says Daniel Rosensweig, chief operating officer of Yahoo! "People want to use the internet whenever they want, how they want and for whatever they want."

Yahoo! is not alone in defining its strategy as working out what its customers (260m unique users every month) are looking for, and then trying to give it to them. The first thing they want is to become better informed about products and prices. "We operate our business on that belief," says Jeff Bezos, Amazon's chief executive. Amazon became famous for books, but long ago branched out into selling lots of other things too; among its latest ventures are health products, jewellery and gourmet food. Apart from cheap and bulky items such as garden rakes, Mr Bezos thinks he can sell most things. And so do the millions of people who use eBay.

And yet nobody thinks real shops are finished, especially those operating in niche markets. Many bricks-and-mortar bookshops still make a good living, as do flea markets. But many record shops and travel agents could be in for a tougher time. Erik Blachford, the head of IAC's travel side and boss of Expedia, the biggest internet travel agent, thinks online travel bookings in America could quickly move from 20% of the market to more than half. Mr Bezos reckons online retailers might capture 10%—15% of retail sales over the next decade. That would represent a massive shift in spending.

How will traditional shops respond? Michael Dell, the founder of Dell, which leads the personal-computer market by selling direct to the customer, has long thought many shops will turn into showrooms. There are already signs of change on the high street. The latest Apple and Sony stores are designed to display products, in the full expectation that many people will buy online. To some extent, the online and offline worlds may merge. Multi-channel selling could involve a combination of traditional shops, a printed catalogue, a home-shopping channel on TV, a phone-in order service and an e-commerce-enabled website. But often it is likely to be the website where customers will be encouraged to place their orders.

One of the biggest commercial advantages of the internet is a lowering of transaction costs, which usually translates directly into lower prices for the consumer. So, if the lowest prices can be found on the internet and people like the service they get, why would they buy anywhere else?

One reason may be convenience; another, concern about fraud, which poses the biggest threat to online trade. But as long as the internet continues to deliver price and product information quickly, cheaply and securely, e-commerce will continue to grow. Increasingly, companies will have to assume that customers will know exactly where to look for the best buy. This market has the potential to become as perfect as it gets.

◎ Useful Words

valuation	[ˌvæljuˈeɪʃən]	n.	评价,估价;计算
dwarf	[dwɔːf]	v.	使矮小
		adj.	矮小的
integral	[ˈɪntɪgr(ə)l; ɪnˈtegr(ə)l]	adj.	积分的;完整的,整体的;必需的
		n.	积分;部分;完整
dime	[daɪm]	n.	一角硬币
lexicon	[ˈleksɪk(ə)n]	n.	词典,辞典
oblige	[əˈblaɪdʒ]	v.	迫使,强制;赐,施恩惠;责成
		v.	帮忙,施恩惠
arbitrage	[ˈɑːbɪtrɪdʒ; ˌɑːbɪˈtrɑːʒ]	n.	套汇,套利;仲裁
fickle	[ˈfɪk(ə)l]	adj.	浮躁的;易变的,变幻无常的
gourmet	[ˈɡʊəmeɪ]	n.	美食家
		adj.	菜肴精美的
fraud	[frɔːd]	n.	欺骗;骗子;诡计

IV. Practicing

1. Match the English words and phrases with the proper Chinese meanings.

(1) order processing　　　　　　　　a. 移动商务

(2) asset services　　　　　　　　　b. 资产服务

(3) electronic data interchange　　　c. 代理商

(4) mobile commerce　　　　　　　　d. 条形码

(5) bar code　　　　　　　　　　　　e. 优惠券

(6) exclusive dealing　　　　　　　　f. 直销

(7) agent middleman　　　　　　　　g. 独家销售

(8) coupon　　　　　　　　　　　　h. 订单处理

(9) post-purchase service　　　　　i. 售后服务

(10) direct selling　　　　　　　　　j. 电子数据交换

Unit 8　E-commerce

2. Fill in the blanks in the following passage with the following words and try to understand what E-commerce is.

| wonderful | present | enormous | electronically |
| responsive | electrically | remarkable | e-commerce |

E-commerce

　　No aspect of e-business has attracted more attention than _____. The ability to offer goods and services over the Web has already had a _____ impact. Last year, for instance, over $750 million in airline tickets were sold over the web. By using e-commerce solutions, companies can _____ their goods more effectively, take orders and invoice online, automate customer account enquiries and handle transactions _____. Not only does this mean improved margins for you, but it also means your customers receive the faster, more _____ service they demand.

(from www.ibm.com)

3. Translate the following English words and phrases into Chinese.
　(1) Application Service Provider _____
　(2) Business Intelligence Services _____
　(3) Corporate Messaging Services _____
　(4) DB2 Universal Database _____
　(5) administered vertical marketing systems _____
　(6) deceptive advertisements _____
　(7) general merchandise discount chain _____
　(8) industry value chain _____
　(9) Customer Relationship Management Services _____
　(10) point-of-sales (POS) data _____

V. Optional Reading

Chinese E-commerce

　　2012-11-21 06:38:00 GMT2012-11-21 14:38:00 (Beijing Time) SINA.com

　　An article published in the Business section of Nov.17 edition of *The Economist* talks about the booming e-commerce in China, here is what it says:

　　It is "one of the few bright spots in the Chinese economy," says Zeng Ming. He is talking about e-commerce. Mr Zeng, the chief strategy officer for Alibaba, a giant Chinese Internet firm, predicts that digital transactions on his firm's platforms will top 1 trillion yuan ($159 billion) this year—more than Amazon's and eBay's combined. That is a bold claim but considering what happened on Singles Sunday.

Invented a few years ago by students and seized upon by digital marketers, this festival for lonely hearts falls annually on the 11th day of the 11th month (since 1 is the loneliest number). It is like St Valentine's Day, only worse, singletons shower each other with tender gifts: a barrage of pearls, a storm of sweets.

This November 11th they spent a staggering 19 billion yuan on Alibaba's online platforms—a fourfold increase on a year ago, and more than double what Americans spent online last Cyber Monday (the Monday after Thanksgiving, when retailers urge Americans to shop online). More than 100m purchases were logged, accounting for 80% of the packages shipped that day. Couriers were buried in parcels.

So life is good for China's e-tailers, then? Not exactly. The number of digital marketers is increasing and online sales are booming. Consumers are enjoying lower prices, better service and more variety. The problem? The pressure on margins in Chinese e-commerce is worse than in America, reckons Elinor Leung of CLSA, a broker. "Almost no one makes money," she says.

The fiercest battles are being fought between online retailers and their bricks-and-mortar rivals. Dangdang, a firm that resembles Amazon, and 360buy（京东商城）, another online retailer, have cut prices ferociously. Tencent, a cash-rich online giant known for its instant-messaging software, is splashing out to win market share. 360buy has also just raised $400m from investors to do the same. But it is unclear how much longer such firms can burn through capital.

That is especially so since physical retailers are fighting back. Walmart has increased its stake in Yihaodian, a local e-commerce firm. Jeff Walters of BCG, a consultancy, argues that in a good year a retailer like Walmart could open 40—50 physical stores, just a sliver of the Chinese market, "which is why e-commerce is so important for them here". Many Western rivals have flopped in China with the big-box strategy; including, most recently, Best Buy（百思买）(an electronics chain) and Home Depot（家得宝）(a do-it-yourself shop).

Suning and Gome, big Chinese high-street electronics stores, are putting an expanded range of products on their websites. Alan Lau of McKinsey & Co, a consultancy, says they are also pushing manufacturers to stop offering e-tailers such big discounts. He estimates that in 2011 computers and handsets sold online were 12% cheaper than in stores; this year they are only 7% cheaper. As the gap gets smaller, so do nearly everyone's margins.

The great exception is Alibaba, which handles nearly three-quarters of China's e-commerce. Because its Taobao and Tmall platforms connect buyers and sellers, the firm does not carry the cost of logistics or inventory. It makes none of the products it sells. It makes money chiefly through advertisements, not user fees, a model that works thanks to its dominant position.

Unit 8　E-commerce

　　Alibaba is bullish. In China e-commerce already accounts for nearly 5% of total retail sales, roughly the same as in America. But its potential is greater, argues the firm. In America, physical retailers are already efficient and everywhere. In China, they are highly fragmented, inefficient and barely visible outside big cities. So e-tailers could leapfrog them.

　　Mr Zeng notes that legions of Chinese have yet to go online. As they do so, Alibaba will be watching, recording and analysing their shopping habits. The firm is devising a "big data" strategy. It hopes to help vendors harness customer information quickly and share insights among themselves. This could allow them to accelerate product-design cycles.

　　The firm's lofty ambition is to help China move towards "mass customisation" and "user-generated innovation"—turning trendy jargon into reality. "The entire supply chain will sit on e-commerce," insists Mr Zeng. "It will be not just a tool, but the heart of the entire economy."

Unit 9 Business Meeting

Unit Aims

- To know the procedures of business meetings
- To learn business meeting discussion strategies
- To grasp useful words and expressions of business meeting
- To know the basic knowledge of minutes and agendas
- To know the basic etiquette of business meetings

Warming Up

Preparation is crucial for a successful meeting. Suppose you are a secretary in a company and preparing for a meeting to be held next week. What should you do before the meeting? Talk about the following activities with your partner and choose the ones that should be carried out by secretaries.

- Consult with the chairperson on the order of business for the meeting on the agenda.
- Ensure that the notice of the meeting is given.
- Circulate to all members (a) any papers to be discussed at the upcoming meeting and (b) a copy of the agenda, minutes of the previous meeting.
- Make sure that any reports or information requested at the last meeting is available.
- Study out the topic of the meeting.

I. Setting up and Canceling Meetings

Read the following two dialogues and pay attention to the key phrases and expressions when setting up and canceling meetings.

Dialogue One

A: Hi, Alex, I'm calling to arrange for a meeting next week. Can you make it Tuesday or

Unit 9 Business Meeting

Thursday afternoon?
B: Tuesday will be OK. What time?
A: What about 2 o'clock. By the way, the meeting will be held in the conference room.
B: OK. Thank you.

Dialogue Two

A: Good morning, Alex. I'm truly sorry but I have to cancel the meeting for Friday. Something has come up at work. I just can't make it.
B: Oh, do you want to reschedule the meeting?
A: If it is convenient, any day next week except Friday would suit me.
B: OK. I have no objection. What about next Tuesday afternoon?
A: Yes, let's make it at 2 o'clock Tuesday afternoon.
B: All right, that's settled.

> **Tips**
>
> Sometimes things come up that are out of our control, so cancelling meetings is just a part of life. One thing we should keep in mind is that when you have to cancel a meeting, you should inform others punctually and politely, and apologize and ask for their understanding sincerely.

◎ Useful Expressions

◎ *When arranging a meeting you might say:*
Can you make Tuesday?
I could make it at 2 o'clock.
◎ *When canceling a meeting you might say:*
I'm afraid I will not make it to our meeting due to a problem that just came up at work.
Unfortunately, an issue just came up at work, and I cannot make it to our meeting this afternoon.
I apologize for the inconvenience, but I am not going to be able to make it to the meeting tomorrow.
◎ *When rescheduling a meeting you might say:*
I need to reschedule our meeting because... (Problem)
I will need to postpone our meeting... (Explain problem)
◎ *When giving alternative dates or times you might say:*
Could we meet tomorrow at the same time?
Are you available on Friday at 2 PM?

Next week is completely open for me. Please let me know the best time for you.

But I've got a tight schedule tomorrow. I might not be able to make it tomorrow. What about...?

II. Meeting Procedure

Knowing about the meeting procedure will help you gain an overall understanding of what happens during a business session or meeting. So when you go to a meeting you will have an idea of what is going on or what stage you are at during a meeting.

1. Opening

Once everyone has arrived, the chairperson, or whoever is in charge of the meeting should formally welcome everyone to the meeting and thank the attendees for coming.

Sample Welcome

- Well, since everyone is here, we should get started.
- Hello, everyone. Thank you for coming today.
- I think we'll begin now. First I'd like to welcome you all.
- Thank you all for coming at such short notice.
- I really appreciate you all for attending today.
- We have a lot to cover today, so we really should begin.

2. Introducing

If anyone at the meeting is new to the group, or if there is a guest speaker, this is the time when introductions should be made. The person in charge of the meeting can introduce the new person, or ask the person to introduce him or herself.

Sample Introduction

- I'd like to take a moment to introduce our new tour coordinator.
- I know most of you, but there are a few unfamiliar faces.
- Stella, would you like to stand up and introduce yourself?
- Hi everyone. I'm Judy Strauss. I'll be acting as Amanda's assistant while Nancy is away on maternity leave.

3. Roll Call/Apologies

If the meeting is a small group, it is probably unnecessary to take attendance out loud. The person who is taking the minutes will know everyone personally and can indicate who is present and who is absent. In a larger meeting, it may be necessary to send around an attendance sheet or call out names. If an important figure is absent, it may be necessary for the chairperson to apologize for his or her absence and offer a brief explanation for it.

Sample Apology

- Unfortunately, Ken cannot join us today. He has been called away on business.
- Mike will be standing in to take the minutes today, as Lisa is home with the flu.
- I'm afraid.., (name of participant) can't be with us today. She is in...
- I have received apologies for absence from (name of participant), who is in (place).

4. Approval of the Last Meeting's Minutes

The approvals of the last meeting's minutes are all very important steps in a meeting. So there should be a section specifically for any matters that arise concerning the last meeting's minutes. Usually, members who were absent from the last meeting will have some points to bring up.

Samples

To begin with I'd like to quickly go through the minutes of our last meeting.

5. Introducing the Agenda

Some people who hold meetings prefer to pass around copies of the agenda, and others will post a large copy on a wall, or use an overhead projector. No matter which format is used, attendees should be able to follow the agenda as the meeting progresses. Before beginning the first main item on the agenda, the speaker should provide a brief verbal outline of the objectives.

Sample Introduction to the Agenda

- So, if there is nothing else we need to discuss, let's move on to today's agenda.
- Shall we get down to business?
- There are X items on the agenda. First, ... second, ... third, ... lastly, ...

6. Allocating Roles (secretary, participants)

Anyone, including you, may be assigned to take the minutes at a meeting. Often someone who is not participating in the meeting will be called upon to be the minute-taker.

Sample Allocation

- (name of participant), would you mind taking the minutes?
- (name of participant) has kindly agreed to give us a report on ...

7. Agreeing on the Ground Rules for the Meeting (contributions, timing, decision-making, etc.)

To make sure that everyone feels open to contribute during meetings, that decisions are made in the best interest of the organization, and all attending are respectfully treated as true team members who are essential to the decision-making process. Establishing ground rules will lay the framework for positive personal interaction and better group decisions.

Samples

- We will hear a short report on each point first, followed by a discussion round the table.
- The meeting is due to finish at...
- We'll have to keep each item to ten minutes. Otherwise we'll never get through.
- We may need to vote on item 5, if we can't get a unanimous decision.

8. Introducing the First Item on the Agenda

Samples

- So, let's start with...
- Shall we start with...
- So, the first item on the agenda is ...
- Pete, would you like to kick off?
- Martin, would you like to introduce this item?

9. Closing an Item

Samples

- I think that covers the first item.
- Shall we leave that item?
- If nobody has anything else to add,

10. Next Item

Samples

- Let's move onto the next item.
- The next item on the agenda is...
- Now we come to the question of...

11. Giving Control to the Next Participant

Samples

- I'd like to hand over to Mark, who is going to lead the next point.
- Right, Dorothy, over to you.

12. Summarizing

Samples

- Before we close, let me just summarize the main points.
- To sum up, ...
- In brief,
- Shall I go over the main points?

13. Finishing Up

Samples

- Right, it looks as though we've covered the main items.
- Is there any other business?

14. Suggesting and Agreeing on Time, Date and Place for the Next Meeting

Samples

In the closing remarks, the chairperson, or participants may want to discuss the date and time for the next meeting, when the minutes will be available, or when a decision should be made by. This is also the time to give contact information, such as how to send a question by e-mail or who to call regarding a certain issue.

- Can we fix the next meeting, please?
- So, the next meeting will be on... (day), the ... (date) of... (month) at...
- What about the following Wednesday? How is that?
- If anyone has any questions about anything we discussed today, feel free to send me an e-mail.
- The minutes from today's meeting will be posted as of tomorrow afternoon.
- I'll send out a group e-mail with the voting results.

15. Thanking Participants for Attending and Congratulations

The end of the meeting is also the time to thank anyone who has not been thanked at the beginning of the meeting, or anyone who deserves a second thank you. Congratulations or Good-luck can also be offered here to someone who has experienced something new, such as receiving a promotion.

Samples
- I'd like to thank Marianne and Jeremy for coming over from London.
- Before I let you go let's all give a big thank you (everyone claps) to Thomas for baking these delicious cookies.
- Again, I want to thank you all for taking time out of your busy schedules to be here today.
- Thanks for your participation.

16. Closing the Meeting

There are different reasons why a meeting comes to an end. Time may run out, or all of the items in the agenda may be checked off. Some meetings will end earlier than expected and others will run late. A meeting may be cut short due to an unexpected problem or circumstance. Here are a variety of ways to adjourn a meeting:

Samples
- The meeting is closed.
- I declare the meeting closed.
- If no one has anything else to add, then I think we'll wrap this up.
- I'm afraid we're going to have to cut this meeting short. I've just been informed of a problem that needs my immediate attention.

III. Meeting Discussions

Read the following dialogue and pay attention to the discussion strategies.

Grace: OK, let's call the meeting to order. You've all looked at the reports given to you a few days ago. I've asked Sam, as marketing director, to lay out the main points of the agenda today. Sam?

Sam: Thanks Grace. Well, let me bring your attention to what I see as the main issues. First are the laws in Central and South America. Will they make it hard for us to do business there? Second is how to sell in that market. Should we try to sell by ourselves? Or should we get people there to sell for us? Yes, Grace.

Grace: As you know, we've asked a legal expert to come today. He isn't here yet, so I think we should get the show started with the second issue, how to sell in that market.

Sam: Good idea. Does everyone agree? Good. The main problem in the market is poor health conditions. We all know what happened to Nests when they sold their powdered milk in Africa. And we don't want that to happen to us. To address this issue, I'd like to call upon our medical expert, Dr. Vincent Davis, to take the floor. Vincent?

Vincent: In Africa, people had very little clean water. So they put dirty water in with the powder. Many people got sick, and Nests got in trouble because of it.

Grace: Can we find a way to prevent this? Isn't it also very hard to find clean water in Central and South America?

◎ Useful Expressions

◎ Getting the Chairperson's Attention

May I have a word?

If I may, I think...

Excuse me for interrupting.

May I come in?

◎ Giving Opinions

I'm positive that...

I (really) feel that...

In my opinion...

The way I see things...

If you ask me ... I tend to think that...

Unfortunately, I see it differently.

Up to a point I agree with you, but...

(I'm afraid) I can't agree...

Excuse me, I would break in here, I think you are a little too optimistic here.

Sorry to interrupt, you are a bit quick with you conclusion.

◎ **Clarifying**

Let me spell it out...

Have I made that clear?

Do you see what I'm getting at?

Let me put this another way...

I'd just like to repeat that...

◎ **Making a Proposal**

I've outlined three options/alternatives to manage our growth.

What we have to do is quite clear. We need to start with ...

Let me give you some scenarios.

I think that Option B is the best alternative. Option A is ...

The other point I want to make is that ...

I want to make a final point.

◎ **Asking for Opinions**

What do you think, George?

What's your opinion/ thought on that, Martha?

Any thoughts on that?

Any ideas?

IV. Taking Meeting Minutes

Anyone, including you, may be assigned to take the minutes at a meeting. Often someone who is not participating in the meeting will be called upon to be the minute-taker. Read the following passage and learn the basic knowledge about minute-taking at a meeting.

How to Take Meeting Minutes

Business minutes are a vital part of the record keeping performed by companies, particularly corporations. Proper governance requires regular meetings of the board of directors with minutes, prepared to record what was reported, discussed and approved or disapproved during the meetings. Minutes memorialize all the company's important decisions regarding management, changes to the business model, expansion plans, major funding events, mergers and acquisitions.

• Fill in the heading and agenda. The top of the page should carry the document title: Minutes of the Meeting of the Board of Directors. Under the title you should indicate the date, time and location of the meeting. This information should be easy to read because you may find yourself hunting through your meeting minutes looking for a specific date or location. The agenda is another useful bit of information that should be easily seen. It will give you a quick idea of what went on in the meeting without having to read the entire document.

Record the attendees. For a regular meeting where there is a list of members who are expected to attend, indicate who is and who is not at the meeting. Some boards require indications of why members are absent, as membership can be revoked if the member misses a certain number of meetings without a good excuse. Also, record any additional attendees and the reason they are in attendance.

• When the reports are given, record them under the "Reports of Corporate Officers and Department Heads" category. There may be votes taken on suggestions from the floor or approval votes on questions raised in the reports, so make sure to indicate who raised each major question or comment, who moved to accept or reject any suggestions, who seconded the motion and the vote both for and against. Also record whether the motion carried. Officers' reports will include presentation of the minutes, a vote to accept the minutes of the previous meeting, the treasurer's report and any reports of any of the other officers.

Record discussions of any ongoing projects or questions under the "Old Business" category. This is for progress reports on projects, resolution of problems and other follow up on questions raised and votes taken in previous meetings. Again, you will need to carefully record any motions from the floor and the details of discussions and votes.

Record new proposals and announcements under the "New Business" category. This is how new projects, plans, suggestions and questions are entered into the board governing process and new business must be recorded carefully along with the details of motions, questions, discussions and votes.

V. Meeting Agenda

The agenda lies at the heart of the meeting, which is required to keep meetings on track and to indicate to members that will be raised. To put it in another word, the agenda is a list of all items scheduled for discussion at a meeting and the order in which they are to be discussed. The group's secretary, who based it on decisions from the last meeting, create the agenda. The secretary  is responsible for writing the agenda, but any employees could perform the work. The secretary is responsible for putting it together, but does have the authority to add items for the members to discuss. The following is a sample of agenda.

Unit 9　Business Meeting

Stafford Heights Speechcraft Club

Meeting Agenda

Meeting No. 456—Monday 25th May 2002

1. Call to order
   1.1 Welcome guests
   1.2 Opening meeting
2. Apologies for absence
3. Minutes
   3.1 Minutes of previous meeting as circulated
   3.2 Business arising from the minute
4. Correspondence
   4.1 Inwards
   4.2 Outwards
   4.3 Business arising
5. Reports
   5.1 Treasurer's report
   5.2 President's report
   5.3 Vice president-membership report
6. General business
   6.1 Motions on notice
   6.2 Submitted motions
   6.3 Business from the floor
7. Notices
   7.1 Notice of motions
   7.2 Notice of upcoming events
   7.3 Notice of next meeting
8. Close of business

VI. Practicing

1. Match the words in the left column with the meaning in the right column.

(1) Minute　　　　　a. It is used to allow timely communication to a large number of employees or other members of an organization.

(2) Agenda　　　　 b. It's a list of all the items scheduled for discussion at a current meeting, and the order in which they will be discussed.

(3) Memorandum　　c. A notification sent to members of a company, informing them of

		a time, date, and location of a shareholder meeting.
(4) Notice	d.	The written or recorded documentation that is used to inform attendees and non-attendees of the happenings during the meeting.

2. Read the passage in Part IV, and answer the following questions.

(1) According to the passage, how many parts are included in a formal meeting minute?

(2) According to the passage, what should meeting minutes be taken for?

(3) Is it necessary for the minute-taker to record every word of each attendee at the meeting? Please give your reasons.

VII. Optional Reading

10 Rules for Proper Business Meeting Etiquette
by George N. Root III, Demand Media

Adherence to the proper etiquette for a business meeting establishes respect among meeting participants, helps the meeting begin and end on time, and fosters an atmosphere of cooperation. A lack of etiquette and poor planning are two of the main reasons why many business meetings fail, according to business expert Lyndsay Swinton. Teach your employees business meeting etiquette to ensure that your business's meetings are effective.

Arrival

Arrive to the location of the business meeting at least 15 minutes early. This allows you to find a seat and get situated before the meeting starts.

Agenda

The chairperson of the meeting should circulate a meeting agenda to each participant at least one week in advance. Participants should call the chairperson to express any concerns about the agenda at least 48 hours prior to the meeting. The chairperson and concerned participant will then have time to determine if changes need to be made. The agenda should also mention the meeting's start and ending times as well.

Be Prepared

Each participant should come to the meeting with all of the materials and data she will need and an understanding of the meeting topic.

Breaks

Meetings should have a break every two hours. Breaks should be 20 minutes long, and meal breaks should be 30 minutes long.

Attire

The chairperson should indicate what kind of attire is required for the meeting, either business casual or business formal, and participants should follow that rule. A representative listing of the attire would be helpful as participants may have differing views on what business casual and business formal is. For example, when listing the meeting as business formal, you can indicate that a button-down shirt and khaki pants are sufficient.

Speaking

Keep the meeting organized by only speaking when you have the floor. Ask questions during the designated question period, and raise your hand to be recognized by the chairperson as having the floor. Do not interrupt someone while they are speaking or asking a question.

Listen

You may find that many of the questions you have about a topic are answered by the content of the meeting. Listen attentively to the meeting and take notes.

Nervous Habits

Avoid nervous habits such as tapping a pen on the table, making audible noises with your mouth, rustling papers or tapping your feet on the floor.

Cell Phones and Laptops

Turn off your cell phone prior to the start of the meeting. If you are expecting an urgent call, then set your phone to vibrate and excuse yourself from the meeting if the call comes in. Unless laptop computers have been approved for the meeting, turn yours off and lower the screen so that you do not obstruct anyone's view.

Unit 10 Board Meeting

Unit Aims

- To know what the board meeting is
- To know how to hold a board meeting
- To know what the Board of Directors Meeting Rules are
- To know how to take the minutes of a board meeting

Warming Up

- What is the board meeting according to your understanding?
- Do you know how to organize a board meeting? Tell us the procedure of a board meeting in your own words.

I. How to Run a Board of Directors Meeting

A board meeting is a formal meeting of the board of directors of an organization, held usually at definite intervals to consider policy issues and major problems. Presided over by a chairperson (chairman or chairwoman) of the organization or his or her appointee, it must meet the quorum requirements and its deliberations must be recorded in the minutes. Under the doctrine of collective responsibility, all directors (even if absent) are bound by its resolutions.

How to Run a Board of Directors Meeting
By Jennifer Hench

A board of directors governs a business or organization. Directors are typically appointed based upon their expertise, knowledge of the operation and personal interest in the business or organization. Board of directors' meetings occur regularly to address issues and concerns. Run your meetings in an organized and efficient manner.

Here are some instructions:

1. Schedule meetings a year in advance so that all board members can be available.
2. Send the meeting schedule to all board members. Request that they respond as to whether they can attend. Use an email meeting tool so that attendees can respond automatically and have the meeting placed on their calendars.
3. Create an agenda for the meeting and outline the items to be covered. List the times the meeting is scheduled to start and conclude. Provide a list of agenda items that is to be covered during the meeting and allow for extra time at the end of the meeting for discussions related to anything additional that was brought up during the meeting. Send the agendas to all board of director members prior to the meeting so that everyone is well aware of what is to be discussed and everyone can come prepared.
4. Verify on the day of the meeting who will be attending. Keep a list of all responses so that when the meeting begins you can start as soon as everyone who said they were coming has arrived.
5. Make copies of the agenda for the current meeting, as well as the agenda and minutes from the previous meeting to remind members what was discussed. Place the previous agenda, last agenda and minutes from the last meeting at each seat.
6. Place additional handouts and information with the other packets of information. For example, if you will discuss advertising strategy you would make and place copies of current advertising information at each member's seat for review during the meeting. Have handouts for any agenda items that require documentation to be discussed thoroughly.
7. Follow the agenda. Address every issue that is to be discussed, then adjourn.
8. Send board members minutes of the meeting or other documentation outlining everything that was discussed and all action items that need to be addressed.

（文章来源：http://www.ehow.com/）

II. How to Conduct a Board of Directors Meeting

Full compliance with your corporation's by-laws means you must conduct board of directors meetings as those laws prescribe. Members do have control over actions the board takes at these gatherings, but they have much less say about how the meetings proceed. Minutes of the meetings, construed by courts as legal documents, are so significant that, as business consultant

Carter McNamara puts it, "...if it's not in the minutes, it didn't happen."

The following instructions will help you with it:

1. Find out what transpires at a typical board of directors meeting by reviewing a sample agenda at Management Help. Customize this agenda to fit your company's culture and purpose.

2. Appoint someone—usually the board secretary—to take minutes of the meeting. Minutes should contain information recommended by McNamara: company name, date and time of meeting, who called the meeting to order, attendees, the motions made, conflicts of interest that prevent an attendee from voting, abstentions from voting and the reasons given, when the meeting ended and who prepared the minutes.

3. Decide if a quorum—the least amount of members necessary to take action—is present. As the Chicago Lawyers' Committee for Civil Rights Under the Law Handbook suggests, check the by-laws to find out how many members are necessary for a quorum. In most corporations, a simple majority will do. For example, a board with ten members would have a quorum if six were present.

4. Have the board chairman call the meeting to order, as in the sample minutes from Management Help. The secretary should take attendance by calling out the names of board members who respond out loud if they are present.

5. Ask if board members reviewed minutes from the previous meeting and if changes are suggested. Then ask other members if they agree with the changes. Note agreement and disagreement. Then vote on whether the changes should be made. If the majority votes yes, announce that the changes will be made and circulated to all members for approval at the next meeting.

6. Ask committee chairs to report on events since the last meeting. Notice how the sample minutes McNamara refers to shows members describing meetings or events they have attended.

7. Vote on motions made by board members to accomplish a task. Examples of motions are hiring a consultant to write grants, approving check lists and financial statements, and even sending gifts to employees who are out sick.

8. Have board members report "new business," or upcoming events. Are they attending conferences other attendees should know about? Or, are they soliciting advice on a particular issue?

9. Adjourn the meeting and announce the time it was adjourned. Give the date, time and location of the next meeting. Specify whether the board will continue meeting in "executive" session where non-board members are not permitted.

（文章来源：http://www.ehow.com/）

III. Board of Directors Meeting Rules

When the board of directors for an organization meet, be it a for-profit corporation or a non-profit organization, the meeting follows a strict set of rules. These rules are designed to give the meetings structure, and stream-line important business through set procedures. While the individual nuances of each rule structure varies with each individual organization, the rules for conducting a board meeting are generally the same, and conform with the entity's bylaws.

Agenda

The foundation for a board's rules regarding meetings are written down in an agenda. The agenda is a formalized plan of what topics are to be addressed during the meeting, the time allotted for each topic and appropriate actions that can be taken during each meeting segment. Adherence to this agenda helps ensure a productive, orderly meeting.

Leadership

It's important for a board to have an experienced leader. The chairperson of the board is typically an experienced, senior member of the board, and should be well versed in parliamentary procedures. Some boards alternate who is chairing, or simply let the most senior member officiate. However, it is best that a chairperson be appointed to always lead the meetings, and that they be experienced in running board meetings and capable of commanding the attention of the board.

Minutes

One of the principle rules in a board meeting relates to the taking of minutes. The minutes of the board meetings are a written record of the meetings themselves, a hard copy of everything said and all business discussed. These minutes are important not only for future meetings, when accurate information from previous meetings might be necessary, but also to establish corporate accountability. With a written record of all board business, there is little deniability for corporate malfeasance.

Motions

When the time comes to make a decision, it is typically carried out by a motion. A member makes a proposal, or motion, and the other members of the board vote. If it garners enough votes, the motion passes and is entered into the minutes for future implementation. If not, it is still entered into the minutes as old business. In the event that all members aren't in attendance, the quorum, or minimum number of attending members to proceed with business, may still vote on motions and resolutions. The only exception is if the minimum number of members required by the quorum are not in attendance.

Majority Rule

All major decisions by the board must be approved by at least a majority of board members. In some boards, the vote must be unanimous, or unanimous with dissenters abstaining. In this way, the board can't be dominated by a single member, but rather is a collective effort, with the individual rights of the members protected.

Professionalism

All board members are required to behave in an professional, business-like manner when conducting a meeting. This means saving all comments or discussions, including dissenting opinions or concerns, for their appropriate times. It also means accepting board decisions with grace, even if there is disagreement with the decision being made.

Personal Appearance

While some boards maintain fairly informal standards regarding dress, boards in larger organizations typically employ strict dress codes. These range from business-casual wear to full business-formal ware, depending on the individual boards. Sometimes, these guidelines extend to personal grooming as well, although typically they are wardrobe specific.

（文章来源：http://www.ehow.com/）

IV. Practicing

1. Answer the following questions

(1) What is the function of the agenda?

(2) What kind of person can be appointed as the chairperson?

(3) Why are the minutes so important?

(4) A member makes a proposal, or motion, and the other members of the board vote. Then what rules must be used?

(5) What can be included in an agenda?

(6) What kind of person can be appointed as directors?

2. Role Play

Suppose you are the chairperson of the board, please conduct a board meeting in your own way.

V. Optional Reading

How to Take the Minutes of a Board Meeting

Meeting: Board meeting 2010—11—08

Contents
    1 Board Meeting 2010 Nov. 08
        1.1 Roll Call
            1.1.1 Present
            1.1.2 Absent
            1.1.3 Regrets
        1.2 Agenda
        1.3 Community Working Group
            1.3.1 Specifics about the Group
            1.3.2 Recruitment Process
            1.3.3 Candidate Decision
        1.4 OpenRespect.org
            1.4.1 Basic Information
            1.4.2 Board Discussion
            1.4.3 Board Decision
        1.5 New Legal Guideline
            1.5.1 Basic Information
            1.5.2 Proposal
            1.5.3 Board Discussion
            1.5.4 The Statement to be Added to Our Legal Guidelines
            1.5.5 Votes
            1.5.6 Board Decision
        1.6 Fedora Elections Process
        1.7 Next Meeting

Board Meeting 2010 Nov. 08
Roll Call
Present
    Tom "spot" Callaway
    Rex Dieter
    Jared Smith

Máirín Duffy

Jon Stanley

Matt Domsch

Colin Walters

Chris Tyler

Absent

(None)

Regrets

Christopher Aillon

Stephen Smoogen

Agenda

Updates

F14 shipped! Hooray! Now let's get to work on F15

Board Business:

#82: Draft a charter for a Community Working Group (https://fedorahosted.org/board/ticket/82)

http://openrespect.org—Does the Fedora Board agree with this statement?

#86: New Legal Guideline (https://fedorahosted.org/board/ticket/86)

Fedora Elections Process

Community Working Group

Specifics about the group

Wiki page: https://fedoraproject.org/wiki/Fedora_Community_Working_Group

Tasks for the group

Will need to come up with code-of-conduct

Come up with proposal to enforce (if deemed needed)

Group will have 5 members

Time duration:

Limited time span, like Board—1 year lifetime.

jds2001 talked to Jeff Mitchell in KDE group, said it is not a big time sink.

Recruitment Process

Karsten doesn't want to join, but wants to be an insider journalist for the Open Source Way

That's fine by us, no opposition—notes need to be sensitive to private meeting content, however.

Everyone else contacted, one interested, rest not interested, or not interested in being a direct member of the group.

Candidate Decision

How to select candidates? We talked about letting Rex select them or having the Board vote, and decided to have a Board vote.

Unit 10 Board Meeting

Decision: We voted for 5 candidates + 1 alternate amongst the nominations we received. These candidates will be contacted. In the case where one of the candidates cannot serve, the alternate will be called on. The candidates will be announced at some future point when they have been confirmed.

OpenRespect.org

Basic Information

Joint statement between Linux distros about respecting each other & communicating in a friendly/civil manner at http://openrespect.org

Jono Bacon wrote it.

Jono Bacon talked to Jared about this, and said he would draft a statement and would involve Jared but ended up releasing via his blog without collaborating before release and emailed Jared afterwards.

Board Discussion

On first glance seems reasonable; what's the effect of having this out there? So what? (ctyler)

KDE community member Aaron Seigo weighs in and decides not to "sign" http://aseigo.blogspot.com/2010/11/commonality-and-community.html

Makes the point that respect is earned. Be cordial & polite to folks you don't know. There's a difference between being polite and respectful (spot)

Jono's Blog post on it: http://www.jonobacon.org/2010/11/05/making-our-world-more-respectful/

Tends to be slanted towards not "picking on" Canonical; the spin makes me uncomfortable (spot)

Fab's comment on Jono's blog post points out difference between respecting people and respecting companies (mizmo)

Can have difference of opinion and still be polite (but respect? not necessarily) (jsmith & jds2001)

At the EtherPad FAD, someone tried to "teach" Spot about licensing... Spot had to be polite & nice... but didn't feel he respected his point of view. Made every effort to be polite & cordial. Was that respectful? Maybe not, but 125% trying to be polite and not saying anything hurtful. There is a difference... if you disagree with someone who has lots of well-research reasons for a different standpoint, still can be respected. (spot)

Don't see inclusion of legitimate criticism... that would be another concern about how this is shaped (ctyler)

Engaging honest, open, and polite debate. Does debate count as criticism or is it okay? (rdieter)

Statement seems to be anti-critcism. Hard time accepting as—is in that case rdieter)

Think the statement should be about civility, not respect (mizmo) (spot +1)

Not sure (a) why this is necessary (b) what do we get from being a part of it? (mdomsch)

All the communities in FLOSS struggling to deal with these issues, maybe could be part of the discussion but not the endpoint (ctyler ?)

Concern: What about new guys (or gals) without a track record? How can they be counted too? (mdomsch)

respect is an aspect of new folks coming in, but courtesy & patience are probably more applicable. if you show a new person courtesy & patience, they have a chance to tackle the problems & earn respect (spot)

"respect" has a lot of different meanings... having respect for someone is different than being disrespectful (spot)

openantidisrespect.org (rdieter)

Board Decision

How do we move forward? Say we don't approve it? Make wording change suggestions? Ignore what he's doing and do our own thing? (jsmith)

Decision: Say we don't approve of the statement and would like to be involved earlier on similar efforts? (Spot)

Decision: Can we ask jono to go back to the problem statement and solicit some brainstorm / ideas (from various FLOSS projects) on how to solve the problem? (mizmo)

Decision: Point out a focus on civility as opposed to respect. (Rex, mizmo+1)

Idea: Could be cool to have a portal that points to various FLOSS projects' statements/policies/codes-of-conducts? <= at least then the website would serve an actual purpose :-p (mizmo)

New Legal Guideline
Basic Information

SQLninja package review request submitted. All that it does is try to exploit vulnerabilities in SQL queries to give you root access on remote systems / root equivalent on Windows systems. (Package request: https://bugzilla.redhat.com/show_bug.cgi?id=637402)

Argument for SQLninja to be added to Fedora is that it is a "penetration testing tool."

Where is the line between what we would take into Fedora b/c it is free software vs. how hazardous it might be?

We never had an explicit policy on this; wanted to wait until we actually encountered it.

RH Legal:

Want us to add some text (text in ticket 86)—gives us another loophole to add to the legal guidelines so we have the right to say the app is too risky / too likely to be used for illegal/dangerous reasons. So we can have some discretion over what is included.

We do bear some additional risk from carrying a tool like this—hacker can claim he didn't know about the tool before we made it visible to him. Not terribly likely but concerning.

Unit 10 Board Meeting

Proposal

Spot proposes we add the new legal text, and also would like us to decide on what to do about SQLninja in particular.

Board Discussion

Just bc you give someone a gun, it doesn't mean they aren't going to shoot someone with it. (jds2001)

This is advertised as "get root on remote systems"—it doesn't advertise itself as a security tool. (spot)

Does it matter what they market themselves as? (colin)

What about the Mozilla extension that creates webtraffic and logs you into websites... might be instructive to know what Mozilla's guidelines for extensions are. (colin)

Wasn't distributed by Mozilla, was distributed by developers

Does the benefit of this app outweigh the risk? (Spot)

Talked to a couple of folks who work in security, and they said having tools like this easily accessible is useful for them. However, is that the primary use case in practice? (spot)

We package Jack the Ripper (mdomsch)

Less concerning because it's not remote/aggressive exploit, need the actual password file from the system. Valid case of oh I forgot the password. (spot)

If legitimate use seems to be more common than not, seems okay to me (spot)

What is the actual risk? (mdomsch)

Really hard to say (spot)

Some legal disclaimer for the software we provide? We can't review everything? (Colin)

Spot asked about disclaiming liability for what people do with the software—Legal said we can do that but it doesn't really do us anything.

for it to be more meaningful, digital signature... CLA won't help because you don't have to be a contributor to use it.

Software creators already disclaiming liability through GPL

Upstream claims SQLninja too complex to set up, so not useful for script kiddies. Has wording like, "Feel free to have fun with this tool, but this might get you in trouble with a lot of law enforcement agencies." (spot)

Who gets the discretion? FESCo? Board? Fedora Legal?

If a legal nature, should be Board (jsmith, Spot) text updated to reflect this

Unfair to submit expostfacto blockers to packages (jds2001)

SQLninja hasn't actually been reviewed yet so it's not ex-postfacto (spot)

The Statement to be Added to Our Legal Guidelines

"Where, objectively speaking, the package has essentially no useful foreseeable purposes other than those that are highly likely to be illegal or unlawful in one or more major jurisdictions in which Fedora is distributed or used, such that distributors of Fedora will face heightened legal risk if Fedora were to include the package, then the Fedora Project Board has discretion to deny inclusion of the package for that reason alone."

Votes

Should we add this text to the Legal guidelines?

    Add the language:++++++

    Don't add language:

Should we approve or deny the SQLninja request in particular?

    Yes, SQLninja is okay to add:

    No, SQLninja shouldn't be added: +++++++

Board Decision

    We will add Spot's proposed langauge to the Fedora legal guidelines. (unanimous)

    We won't allow the SQLninja package to be added to Fedora. (unanimous)

Fedora Elections Process

    Nobody really stepped up to manage

    Chris Tyler has time to step in now

    Symptom of larger problem of heavily—involved folks getting burnt out (mdomsch)

    New Fedora Program manager coming onboard soon, taking over John Poelstra's job. Will be announced via Jared's blog soon. (jsmith)

    Suggestion: Add election coordination to Fedora Program manager job description (spot)

    People didn't know where to submit their answers to the questionnaire—ongoing confusion on the list today

Next Meeting

Friday, November 12th (IRC office hours) Monday, November 15th (Secretary: Smoogen)

（文章来源：https://fedoraproject.org/w/index.php?title=Meeting: Board_meeting_2010-11-08&oldid=206128）